W9-BJJ-086

When the
Breast Fairy
Comes

When the
Breast Fairy
Comes

Understanding and
Communicating
with Your Daughter
during Adolescence

Stacey L. Roberts

CELESTIAL ARTS
Berkeley / Toronto

Copyright © 2002 Stacey Roberts

All rights reserved. No part of this book may be reproduced in any form, except brief excerpts
for the purpose of review, without written permission of the publisher.

Celestial Arts
P.O. Box 7123
Berkeley, California 94707
www.tenspeed.com

Distributed in Australia by Simon & Schuster Australia, in Canada by Ten Speed Press Canada,
in New Zealand by Southern Publishers Group, in South Africa by Real Books, in Southeast
Asia by Berkeley Books, and in the United Kingdom and Europe by Airlift Book Company.

Cover and book design by Nina J. Miller

Roberts, Stacey L.
     When the breast fairy comes: understanding and communicating with your daughter
     during adolescence / Stacey Roberts. -- Rev. ed.
     p. cm.
     Includes bibliographical references and index.
     ISBN 1-58761-162
     1. Teenage girls--Family relationships. 2. Parent and teenager. 3. Self-esteem in
     adolescence. 4. Parenting. I. Title.

HQ798 .R55 2003
649'.133--dc21
     2002041216

Printed in the United States
First printing, 2002

1 2 3 4 5 6 7 8 9 10 — 06 05 04 03 02

Dedication

*This book is dedicated to
all the girls I have coached, counseled, or mentored.
Because of you I was inspired
to write this book.
You have taught me more about life
than you will ever know.*

*In loving memory of
Michelle LePine Deist and Sarah Hegarty*

◎ ◎ ◎

Acknowledgments

There are many people who have helped me to complete this work. First I would like to thank my husband for putting up with the long hours of writing—thank you for your understanding and support. In addition I would like to acknowledge Linda Mead of LitWest Group, L.L.C. for her advice and her belief in the value of this book. Thank you to the many people who reviewed this manuscript and submitted feedback and comments. Thank you to Carrie Rodrigues and those at Ten Speed Press and Celestial Arts who have put great effort into creating a work that will hopefully have a positive impact on those who read it. Thanks also to the mothers, fathers, and daughters who contributed their stories, their voices, and their letters for others to identify with and learn from. Finally, I would like to thank my friends and family for their continued support and encouragement.

Contents

Helping Your Child to Come Up with Her Own Solutions

More Tips, Tricks, and Techniques

The Fatigue Factor

Defuse It, Don't Lose It

Controlling Your Unconscious Reaction

The Art of Apologizing

Adolescent Girls and Stress

Eliminating Unnecessary Stress

What Is Self-Esteem?

The Development of Self-Esteem

Differentiating Self-Esteem, Self-Confidence, and Self-Image

Friend "Shifts" and Self-Esteem

Getting Caught Up in Her Pain

Pain Is Inevitable, Suffering Is Optional

Self-Esteem Issues May Be Difficult to Spot

What Role Does Body Image Play?

What a Parent Can Do

Introduction

The inspiration for the first edition of this book, *When The Breast Fairy Comes: A Parent's Survival Guide for Raising Girls* (2000), came from my observations of and conversations with adolescent girls. While working with girls six days a week, three to four hours a day since 1987, I have witnessed common patterns in adolescent girls' behavior. This revised edition goes a step further by documenting the experiences of adolescent girls and their parents.

This time in a girl's life can be both frustrating and exciting for girls and their parents.

The following pages are filled with personal stories of parents and adolescent girls. These stories often contain advice from experts, parents, and girls themselves that is intended to help prepare others for their journey through adolescence.

All parents and girls experience some difficulty during the adolescent years. Some of the pain is inevitable and some unnecessary. *When the Breast Fairy Comes* will help you understand what your daughter is going through and how you can guide her through the physical and emotional changes she is experiencing.

In these pages, you'll learn how to build a healthy relationship with your daughter during all the stages of adolescence. Effective communication techniques, the stress of parenthood, and the importance of role modeling will be discussed in detail. Self-esteem and its importance to your daughter's development will be discussed, including the factors that lead to high self-esteem.

The warning signs of depression, eating disorders, self-mutilation, and unhealthy relationships will be covered along with what to do if their daughter suffers from any of these problems.

In addition, parents are introduced to skills that will allow them to teach your daughters important life lessons.

Parents have reported that after reading the first edition of this book they feel more in control and ready for their daughter's journey through adolescence. They have insight into their daughter's needs during this very confusing time and know how to handle difficult situations.

In writing this book, I hope to help parents and their daughters go through adolescence with less conflict, better communication, and more understanding. Above all, I am hopeful that this book and its contents encourage parents and their children to stay connected—not just during the teen years, but for life.

Overview of Adolescence

Is your daughter driving you crazy? She won't talk. She won't listen. Your relationship has been chaotic since she started showing signs of puberty. Well, welcome to the wonderful world of adolescence, that challenging time that all girls and their parents must go through. *When the Breast Fairy Comes* emphasizes the importance of staying connected to your daughter in the good and the difficult times. So please, read on and enjoy knowing that you can build on the strengths of your relationship or even repair a damaged one.

What to Expect during Adolescence

In the past, researchers have identified adolescence as the period between the ages of ten and eighteen. Now psychologists are saying that adolescence can begin at age eight and can last until the early twenties.[1] Menstruation has been documented to begin as early as age eight in some cases, and women are facing many issues today in their twenties that in the past were usually resolved by the time they were eighteen. The period of adolescence has grown, and so has its complexities.

Your daughter's adolescence will include many ups and downs for both parent and child. Watching your daughter grow into a young woman can be exciting and rewarding. Parents also often feel frustrated and helpless when they become the target of verbal attacks such as "I hate you" or "I will never be like that when I am a parent." (Your daughter's body may suddenly seem to have been inhabited by some type of alien being. Often a sophisticated form of language accompanies this transformation. This new form of communication involves highly civilized responses, like, "Duh" or "Whatever!" or "Mom (or Dad), you are so weird.")

Are feelings of frustration and helplessness all you can expect during your daughter's journey through adolescence? Definitely not. You will also feel joy and pride at her accomplishments and excitement as she reaches milestones, in addition to worry and confusion over how to handle her more difficult behavior. And though there may be times when you strongly consider sending her to boarding school, parents of daughters in their twenties and thirties have revealed that staying connected with their daughters by attempting to see things from her point of view helped them to develop a long-lasting, loving relationship between parent and child.

In order to establish this kind of positive relationship, it is necessary to prepare yourself. Let's take a look at some of the physical and physiological changes that occur during adolescence.

Physical and Physiological Changes

As a young girl approaches adolescence her body begins to change. As a matter of fact, her body goes through more changes in adolescence than in any other time in life with the exception of the first year. At a certain age, anywhere between eight and thirteen,[2] gonadotropic hormones are released from a gland in the brain called the pituitary. These hormones travel to the ovaries and enable the ovaries to begin producing the hormone estrogen, which, with other hormones, is responsible for the physical changes that occur in a young girl's body.

PHYSICAL CHANGES IN ADOLESCENCE

Body fat increases.

Growth spurts occur.

Body odor becomes pronounced.

Menstruation begins.[3]

Hair in underarms, on legs, and in pubic area becomes more prominent.

Breast buds, or hard lumps around the nipple area begin to form.

Acne develops.

Hips begin to widen.

The First Period

A girl's first menstrual period is an event that she may both anticipate and fear. She may look forward to becoming a woman, especially if her friends feel the same way about their periods, but she may also be afraid or embarrassed of the rather messy physical aspects of menstruation. Talking with your daughter about the physical changes that occur during adolescence will help her prepare for this confusing time. She may be embarrassed and not want to talk about topics such as her first period, but discussions such as the following will help her prepare herself for the natural changes her body will experience.

Parent	Hi, honey! How was your day?
Daughter	It was fine.
Parent	Good. Listen, I'd like to talk to you about something.
Daughter	What?
Parent	This may seem weird to you, but I want to talk with you about becoming a young woman.
Daughter	(Rolling her eyes.) Oh, no, please not a sex talk. We talked about all that stuff in school already.
Parent	Well, sex is only part of it. I want to talk with you about getting your period. Have you discussed menstruation at school or with your friends?
Daughter	Yeah.
Parent	So, what do you think about it?
Daughter	It's gross. That whole thing about getting a period is just disgusting.
Parent	I know it seems disgusting. I felt that way too. But now that I look back on it, I was more afraid of what was going to happen to me than disgusted. I was afraid because I wasn't sure what would happen. I just want to make sure you know what to do so you won't be afraid like I was.
Daughter	Like what?
Parent	We'll talk about that in a minute. But first, do you have any questions?
Daughter	Did it hurt?
Parent	Mine didn't. But some women experience cramps with their first period. Mostly, I was embarrassed. I thought everyone was looking at me. Of course, that wasn't the case. Any other questions?

The average age to begin menstruation is between twelve and thirteen.

Daughter	*I don't know.*
Parent	*OK. Well, shall we put together a plan so you'll know what to do when it happens? For example, if you are in school when you notice your period is starting, what do you think might be good to do?*

Helping your daughter formulate a plan will lessen the anxiety she may have about beginning menstruation.

At times daughters become quite sensitive to their father's comments about their menstruation. Girls may become agitated if their dad asks them about their period or if their mom tells their dad that their daughter has her period. They react this way because they are embarrassed. Girls say they do not want the fact that they have their period broadcast to everyone—they want their privacy.

Frequently dads become embarrassed as well. But there are dads who feel it is important to know what is going on with their daughters and want to be informed, even if it results in a little embarrassment on the part of father or daughter. When you notice your daughter's discomfort about the topic, an effective response from a parent would be "It's a normal, healthy process you are going through. We are glad that you are growing into a woman."

Parents should refrain from making derogatory comments about their daughter's menstruation. "You are really crabby today. Do you have your period?" and similar comments will increase your daughter's emotional discomfort and break down communication. If she is overly sensitive, crabby, or melancholy during her period, a conversation such as this one might allow your daughter to become more conscious of her emotions and how they are affecting her behavior. It's best to start this type of discussion at a time when your daughter is not feeling particularly crabby or sensitive.

Parent	*I've noticed that you are not quite yourself lately. Is there something that we can help you with?*
Daughter	*What? I'm fine. Why are you always on my back?*
Parent	*I'm glad you're fine. But have you noticed that when you have your period you act a little differently?*
Daughter	*I don't know. Maybe.*
Parent	*It's common to feel different around the time that you have your period. Many hormonal changes happen inside your body when you have your period. But the fact that you are not feeling well is not an excuse to treat people poorly. Do you agree?*
Daughter	*I don't know. I guess. I just don't seem to be able to control what I am saying—it just comes out.*

The fact that your daughter feels that her emotions are out of control provides an opportunity for you to let her know that she is in charge of her emotions and behavior, not the other way around. You can tell her that she is responsible for her actions and her state of mind, and this may give her the confidence she'll need to deal with difficult situations in the future. See chapter 2 for more information on communicating with your daughter.

The Breast Fairy Visits

Breast development is one of the obvious physical changes a girl experiences as she enters adolescence. The breast buds appear around the time when a young girl starts menstruating. The buds are usually hard underneath the nipple area, which is a concern to some parents and their daughters but is most often a normal part of development. Itchiness in the area of the budding breasts is common. The initial development period varies depending on the child. But what may not be as obvious to you are your daughter's feelings about her breasts. She may be anxiously awaiting the Breast Fairy, or she may be quietly hoping that no one will notice her arrival. Depending on your daughter's outlook, you may or may not have to prompt her to purchase her first bra.

The First Bra

The trip to make this purchase can be an exciting time for a young woman, or it can seem horrifying to her. One mom remembers her daughter's fear that someone from her school would see her at the store and notice that she was purchasing a bra. The girl quickly grabbed the first bra her mother showed her, bunched it up into a ball, and placed it in the cart underneath the rest of the articles so no one could see it. Attempting to understand your daughter's feelings and reactions and encouraging her to talk about these feelings will help you see things from your daughter's point of view. This is also an important step toward developing effective communication, which will strengthen your relationship in the years to come.

> Scientists and parents have observed the growth of a new appendage during adolescence that seems to be associated with hormonal changes. This appendage appears as an extension of the ear and is usually referred to as "the telephone."

Excellent resources for young girls to find out more about their maturing bodies are found on the Web at www.kidshealth.org and www.youngwomanshealth.com. Books such as *What's Happening to My Body?* by Lynda Madaras explain the changes your daughter's body undergoes during adolescence.

Emotional Changes

The emotional changes that accompany the physical metamor-phosis of adolescence are partly the result of hormones. These changes continue through early, middle, and late adolescence and vary depending on the individual. Mood swings and exces-sive highs and lows are common among adolescent girls.[4] Who knew part of this difficulty was the result of raging hormones?

Adolescence can be both the most fun and the loneliest of times. "Sometimes I sit and cry alone in my room for no reason at all and then ten minutes later I am talking on the phone to my friend and laughing hysterically. This drives my mom crazy," says a thirteen-year-old. In addition to mood swings the adolescent develops what many parents call "the attitude," which includes self-centeredness. Dr. Maria Montessori, the creator of the Montessori method of education, states that pat-terns of behavior in adolescence are similar to the patterns of behavior of a three-to-six-year-old child, who also tends to be very self-centered. Young children and teenagers alike may utter such comments as "This is mine!" and "I want to do it myself!" Both the adolescent and the three-to-six-year-old want to experience situations without their parents. The young child, though, wants the parent to be near at all times, whereas the adolescent wants the parent to be available, but usually not nearby.

Self-absorption is also a normal part of adolescence. Many times it does not even occur to the adolescent that other people have a life outside of their relationship with her. A parent may become irritated at their daughter because she never asks how their day went or never seems to care what her siblings did dur-ing the day. As difficult as it may be for a parent to understand, this is typical behavior for adolescent girls.

During this stage, occasionally ask your daughter how she would feel if someone acted this way toward her. Consistently (but not constantly) remind her that others make sacrifices for her and that it is important for her to show her appreciation; this is one technique that has helped some parents and daughters get through this trying stage while maintaining a close relationship.

You may find yourself becoming angry at your daughter and wanting to tell her that she is selfish. Try to refrain from calling her names, however. Katrina, a sixteen-year-old, wrote this to her mom: "When you call me selfish it really hurts, and to be honest it makes me want to act more selfish toward you. I don't think I am selfish and neither do my friends. Why do you have to call me names?"

Katrina probably does show signs of selfishness in some situations at home, but she obviously does not feel that she is a selfish person. Her mom calling her selfish seems to evoke an "I'll show you" attitude. Katrina reacts to her own hurt feelings by acting even more selfish when her mom is around. When asked why she doesn't talk to her mom about this issue Katrina states, "I don't know. I guess I'm afraid she'd be even madder if I brought it up. Besides, she wouldn't listen anyway."

Another technique that is useful when dealing with a self-absorbed adolescent is to role model the desired behavior. If parents model being genuinely interested in the lives of others, then the adolescent is likely to pick up this behavior eventually.

Emotional Immaturity

Author Theodore Lidz describes adolescence as "a time of turbulent awakening to love and beauty but also of days darkened by loneliness and despair . . . the adolescent lives with a vibrant sensitivity that carries to ecstatic heights and lowers to almost untenable depths."[5] What an adult may perceive as something silly or insignificant can send a teen into a frenzy. Teens live in the moment and experience highs and lows very quickly and sporadically. Mary Pipher, author of *Reviving*

Ophelia, explains that a girl's ability to handle an adverse situation is limited because she lacks the experience needed to rationalize.[6] In addition, many times an adolescent girl will display all-or-nothing behavior. For example she may say, "No one likes me." "All my teachers hate me." "Everyone else gets to go out on a school night." Dealing with this behavior can be difficult for you. If you do not realize that this is typical adolescent behavior, you may worry that you are being too hard on her.

DEALING WITH SELF-ABSORPTION
Expect self-centered behavior.
Avoid calling your daughter selfish.
Model desired behavior.
Periodically remind your daughter that others matter too.

One parent comments, "Sometimes I feel like such a jerk. According to my daughter everyone else can go out on a school night or watch a television show that I feel is inappropriate except her. Am I being too strict or old-fashioned?"

Emotional Roller Coaster

The adolescent girl is on the continuum between child and adult, and her place on that continuum can change in a matter of minutes depending on the situation. Consider this story: Fifteen-year-old Cindy and her teacher were having a conversation about AIDS and the effects this disease has had around the world. Cindy's teacher was impressed at the maturity of Cindy's comments on the subject. However, within ten minutes of this conversation the teacher noticed Cindy giggling with two of her friends about a boy who had just walked past them in the hallway.

Another parent comments, "My thirteen-year-old daughter can be laughing hysterically and ten minutes later when I ask her a question she sobs uncontrollably. And an hour later she is fine and looks at me like I have the problem."

Note: Although these ups and downs may be frequent and typical of the adolescent girl, parents should become familiar with the behavioral warning signs so they can detect when their daughter may be suffering from feelings of depression or other problems, which can lead to serious disorders and even suicide. These red flags are discussed in chapter 8.

Emotional Intimacy

Emotional intimacy is evident throughout adolescence. The adolescent girl is constantly searching for a friend with whom she can share all her most intimate emotions and ideas. Friendships become the focal point of her life.

What she is really seeking is some-one to lean on so she is not alone. The adolescent girl wants someone she can have fun with and share the excitement of life with. One eighteen-year-old explains, "It's like, you can't talk to your parents about deep stuff because you think they might freak out or something, so you feel like you are out there, kind of alone, I guess. Then you search for that one friend who will like you no matter what you think or feel. It's also cool when she shares things with you because then you know you are not the only one feeling a certain way."

BEHAVIORAL CHANGES TO EXPECT

Frequently disagrees with you

Is embarrassed to be seen with you

Is embarrassed by what you say

Is embarrassed by what you do

Is embarrassed by what you wear

Continually points out when the parent is wrong (which according to her is nearly every time you say something)

Requires privacy (bedroom door closed, bathroom door locked)

Looks at you as though you have just lost your mind

Whispers and giggles on the phone

Rolls her eyes

Physical Intimacy and Sexuality

Due to hormonal changes and development of sexuality, girls are likely to have their first sexual encounter during adolescence. During adolescence, boys become a major focus for some girls. They may experience their first kiss as well as their first situation where they may feel pressure to have intercourse or oral sex.

Hillary, twenty-two, remembers, "This was a really weird time in my life. I really wanted a boyfriend, but when I had one and I had to deal with do we have sex or not, it was such a pain. I knew other girls who would have sex with a guy just so they would have someone to like them. I think that is really sad."

Twenty-year-old Clare comments, "I have to admit, I was really curious about sex and stuff. But at the same time I was really confused. It seemed like when I didn't have a boyfriend, I wished I had one, but then when I did have a boyfriend, well, I wanted to be single again. And the anticipation leading up to sex was so intense, but then when I actually had sex with someone I thought I loved, it was like, 'What was so great about that?'"

Ten-year-old Hanna writes, "All that stuff about boys is gross. The only boy I want in my life is my dad!"

A girl's adolescence is a perfect time for her father to comprehend the importance of his relationship with his daughter. Essentially, the relationship with her father is young girl's first experience with love of the opposite sex. Many times it is this father-daughter relationship that helps the adolescent determine what kind of relationship she will want with an adult partner.[7]

Struggling with Sexuality

Girls may also struggle with their sexuality during adolescence. They may feel pressure to label themselves as heterosexual or homosexual. The entertainment media sends provocative messages to girls and boys, and some boys may pressure girls to become sexually intimate before they are ready. And most girls are simply curious about physical intimacy.

Intense emotional relationships are a normal part of adolescence. Some girls believe they must label themselves as homosexual because they have had intense feelings for another girl, and some girls are petrified that they might be homosexual. However, there is no reason to place a label on themselves at this age. Having strong feelings for the same sex may or may not be an indication that one is homosexual. In fact, sexuality is an aspect of themselves that teens can continue to explore.

Adolescents who are questioning their sexuality have told me that the entire subject is confusing for them. Whenever they turn on the television, watch a movie, or open a magazine they see sex. "It's in my face all the time, so I am curious," they say. Their curiosity draws them to experiment sexually. Maintaining an ongoing discussion with your daughter about physical and emotional intimacy will give her a safe place to talk about issues that are bothering her. Girls have confided to me that even with their friends they do not share everything, especially when they are worried that their feelings may not be "normal."

If parents feel that they cannot talk to their daughter about these issues and are concerned that their daughter is being promiscuous or making unhealthy choices, they should encourage a relationship with an appropriate mentor so that she has someone to talk to about these issues. And if parents are uncomfortable talking about sexuality with their daughter, this may signal the need to explore the reasons for their feelings and learn to become more comfortable with the topic of sexuality and sex so they can better support their daughter.

Developmental Tasks of the Adolescent Girl

One of the tasks of the adolescent girl is to liberate herself from the parental hold. For most girls this is an exciting, confusing, and frightening task, one that contributes to the erratic, unreasonable behavior that is typical of teens.

I prefer to refer to this process as "liberation versus separation"[8] because the word *separation* implies a disconnection, or an end to the relationship. Parents whose relationship with their adolescent girls has consisted of good communication, mutual respect, and unconditional love do not separate from their daughters. On the contrary, these parents seem to stay connected, just in a different way than they had been before. One parent told me, "Providing a safety net for my daughters was key in allowing them to spread their wings and take risks because they knew I would be here if they needed to talk."

Adolescents should be encouraged to liberate themselves, not separate, from their parents. During the process of liberation, the parent-child relationship changes: where teaching through instruction and demands once prevailed, teaching through discussion and by parental example become the primary methods of imparting information. Therefore, when a child liberates herself from her parents with the parents' blessing and support, a connection can remain. This liberation requires a shift in the child-parent relationship to a mutual understanding of each other. The authors of *Mother Daughter Revolution* say it best: "Connection, not separation [from her parents] is what makes a girl strong."[9]

During adolescence a girl's inner being or spirit is developing. Author Theodore Lidz describes adolescence as "seeking inward to find whom one is; and a searching outward to locate one's place in life."[10] These tasks are of the utmost importance in her development. Jenny, a fourteen-year-old, states, "I know I am here on this earth for a reason, but I honestly have no clue what that reason is. I constantly wonder what I should do with my life and where I fit in." Parents often forget that they have asked these very questions of themselves both as a child and as an adult. It is important to remember the questions your daughter has are of great concern to her and shouldn't be trivialized by comments like, "You are just going through a phase." Or "Don't be silly." Jenny continues, "When my mom tells me that I am being silly or that this is just a phase, I just want to scream. It's like she has no idea what I am going through or doesn't really care."

Girls who feel as if their parents understand them say their parents listen to their questions and ideas and encourage them to explore and find the answers to these questions, even when they are not consistent with the parents' point of view. By discouraging or brushing off their daughter's questions, parents send a signal to their daughter that the parent does not understand her. A girl in this situation is less likely to come to her parents with her problems because she is convinced that they will not take them seriously.

Parents often ask me why their daughter listens to other adults instead of to her own parents. To find out, I asked their daughters. These girls, ages fourteen to eighteen explained some of the reasons they felt more comfortable talking with other adults:

The other adult showed that he or she cared about them because they were always willing to listen.

The adult never made fun of what they said or felt, never made them feel unimportant.

They felt they were heard or understood because the adult didn't react by telling them what to do.

They did not feel judged.

They felt the adult gave advice only when asked.

So, you are not crazy and she is not possessed (although at times I am sure you could make a good case for an exorcism). As a parent you have the challenge of staying connected with your daughter through the ups and downs of adolescence. While it may be difficult at times, creating a loving relationship that lasts a lifetime is worth the price that you must pay through these tumultuous years. The basis for this ideal type of parent-child relationship is learning to effectively communicate with your daughter throughout adolescence.

Effectively Communicating
with Adolescents

Let's face it, adolescence is tough. Children feel more stress than ever before. The majority of teens I interviewed told me that they often felt very stressed-out or depressed. Many said that they had thought about suicide.

Sandy, a fourteen-year-old writes, "Sometimes I think my parents just don't care. Every time I get upset they tell me I am making a big deal out of nothing. They tell me that my sister went through the same thing and she did fine. Well, don't they know I am not my sister and just because she got through it doesn't mean I can? It makes me so angry that they won't even listen or care how much this means to me."

In the following pages, I will show communication techniques that have worked for me and for parents of adolescent girls. I'll also discuss what girls say they need from the significant adults in their lives. You will find suggestions for listening, allowing your daughter to be heard, and letting her to come up with solutions to her problems that may be even better than what you would have proposed. Isn't this ultimately what we want for our children? We want them to learn to work through a situation and come up with an appropriate answer on their own, since we are not always going to be there to give advice. When you use empathic listening skills and other effective communication techniques you allow your daughter to make her own decisions, with some help and advice from you. Because she is learning under your supervision, you'll feel better about the decisions she makes when you are not around.

Effective communication on your part can influence your daughter's behavior and help you understand where she is coming from. Often we find it difficult to communicate with people because we only consider our own frame of reference. According to Chris Bolender, a school guidance counselor, if you want to communicate effectively with your adolescent, or with anyone else for that matter, you'll need to attempt to understand what your daughter is saying by learning about her frame of reference. To successfully do this, you may have to change your behavior.

Up to now you were most likely unaware that there might be a problem with the way you communicate. You may have thought that the communication issue was your daughter's fault. Some parents have said, "If she would just listen, then I would not have to get so angry." However, you, the adult, have more life experiences and resources and, therefore, should be the one to consider changing. And try as you might, you will not be able to force your daughter to change. When you realize this and work on communicating effectively instead of trying to change your daughter's behavior, something beautiful is likely to happen in your relationship—your daughter may just follow your lead and change the way she communicates as well, and she may become more accepting of your ideas and advice.

Judith, a parent of three girls, relates, "Before I became aware of how I was communicating with my girls I would simply react angrily to what one of the girls had done or what they had said. I was trying so hard to not be like my own mother, that ironically I was acting like my mother. My message to the girls, I believe, was that they were not important because I rarely considered their position and my voice continually reflected angry feelings that I am only now beginning to know I had. Once I became conscious of the way I was speaking to my daughters I changed my delivery. The same messages that I was trying to get across before with no success were beginning to be heard."

You may find it difficult to change your delivery and become aware of old communication patterns and feelings, because for ten or more years you have been communicating with your daughter and everything has appeared to be fine up to now. But as your daughter enters adolescence and makes the journey toward adulthood, she may not respond in the same way to the communication style you used in the first decade of her life. I have heard time and time again from girls, "My parents still treat me like a baby," "I don't want to talk to them. They won't understand," or, "All my mom does is yell when I ask her something."

Using effective communication gives your daughter the feeling that you are willing to listen to her and are trying to understand what she is going through. Essentially you are showing her that she is important to you. If she does not feel that you will try to understand, or if she thinks that you will lecture her or think less of her, she won't come to you when there is something more serious going on. One seventeen-year-old girl who is in the top 10 percent of her class writes, "I am not afraid of what my parents will do to me if I tell them something. It's more that I think they think I am stupid or can't handle something if I make a mistake. They tell me I can tell them anything, but when I have in the past, I just got yelled at or punished without being able to explain myself. I am convinced they think I am a failure."

Dear Mom and Dad,

This letter is kind of hard to write. I was interviewed for this book and then asked to write a letter about listening. Honestly, I really don't think you ever listen to me. Whenever I come to you with a problem, you usually cut me off and tell me your opinion before I get through telling you my whole problem. It seems like you don't care about what I have to say. Most of our talks end up in fights. I know you think I am disrespectful or spoiled because I heard you guys say that behind my back. I want to tell you all this but for some reason I can't. I wish I knew how.

I just want you to hear my side of things and then maybe you will understand me a little better. I just want you to think that I am important and maybe I have something to say that would surprise you. Maybe you might think I'm smart or something.

When you don't listen I end up doing things that make you mad. I don't know why cuz I will just get in trouble. When you don't listen to me it makes me think you don't love me.

So please, just once listen to what I have to say.

Thanks

Your daughter is changing, and you owe it to her to change the way you communicate with her. Consider the following poem by an anonymous Anglican bishop.[1]

When I was young and free and my imagination had no limits,
I dreamed of changing the world;
As I grew older and wiser I realized the world would not change.
And I decided to shorten my sights somewhat and
change only my country.
But this too seemed immovable.
As I entered my twilight years, in one last desperate attempt,
I sought to change my family, those closest to me
But alas they would have none of it.
And now here I lie on my deathbed and realize
(perhaps for the first time)
That if only I'd changed myself first, then by
Example I may have influenced my family
And with the encouragement and support
I may have bettered my country, and who knows,
I may have changed the world.

I have heard many parents say, "Hey, this is a two-way street. Shouldn't she have to change too? After all, she is the one who is moody and disrespectful." This may be true, but maybe if you change your behavior or your reaction toward her behavior, she'll follow suit and actually listen to you. It's worth a try.

Says one mother, "Just a few days ago my daughter came into my room in the morning before school and wanted to wear shorts in the middle of winter because the news said it was going to be seventy degrees. Before working on how to effectively communicate I would have told her to stop being ridiculous and dress appropriately for winter. She would have stomped out of the room in anger. But this time I changed my voice and got rid of the anger behind it. Softly yet firmly, I suggested to her that she think about wearing warmer clothes to school because seventy degrees in winter doesn't feel the same as seventy degrees in summer. Instead of stomping out of the room, my daughter thought for a moment and simply said, 'Alright, Mom' and left the room without any fuss. I have to admit, I surprised myself."

What Is Effective Communication?

Effective communication skills can be used to help parents influence their daughter's behavior in a positive way. Effective communication consists of two basic elements: role modeling and listening.

Difficulty with parental communication was strongly associated with children feeling less happy, smoking, and drinking alcohol.
1997-98 Survey National Institute of Children's Health and Human Development

Behavior Modeling

Behavior modeling is often overlooked as a form of communication. But it is a highly effective way of influencing your daughter's behavior. Throw the old saying "Do as I say, not as I do" right out the window. It doesn't work. A better saying is "Actions speak louder than words." Without even realizing it, your daughter is learning how to communicate with people every day by watching you. You were your daughter's first source of information. From the moment she was born you were setting an example for your child. When she couldn't speak, she would mimic your movements. When she began to speak, she would mimic both your movements and your words. As a child, you also experienced this subconscious learning. This explains why we sometimes find ourselves saying something our mom or dad once said. We swore we would never say it, but there we are saying exactly the same thing our mom or dad said to us.

During adolescence, as much as she tries to avoid you and wishes you were not around, your child will model your behaviors.

Although she may request that you drop her off a few blocks from school or give you that look that says you know absolutely nothing, causing you to feel that she does not want you or need you anymore, your daughter needs you now more than ever. She often looks to you as a model of behavior, either consciously or subconsciously. And without your realizing it, your daughter picks up differences in the behavior that you are modeling versus the behavior you expect from her.

The following are some comments from adolescent girls that show that daughters are paying attention to their parents' behavior:

"My mom gets so mad at me when I talk to my friends on the phone. I admit, sometimes I talk to them for hours, but so does she. Sometimes she'll be on the phone with her friend for more than an hour, but for some reason, it is not OK for me." Another teen states, "My mom always expects us to be on time. She gets very angry when we are late. But when she is supposed to pick us up somewhere she is never on time and it drives me crazy!" Another teen comments, "My dad always expects me to be polite and respectful toward his friends when they are on the phone or when they come over. But when my friends call he is so rude. He hardly ever talks to them. When they stop over, he rarely looks up over his paper to say hello." Another girl complains, "Whenever my friends and I are talking about someone at our school, my parents always tell us not to talk behind their back. But at the dinner table they are always making fun of someone at work or someone they have seen."

One father remarks, "It is always easy to tell your kids what to do without ever thinking about what you are doing yourself. When they bring it up to you, it seems as though they are being a smart aleck, but, really, they have a point." As a matter of fact, because they want to show that they are not you, adolescents look for and point out these inconsistencies in your behavior.

When your actions are consistent with the behavior you expect of your children they learn the correct behavior in two ways—by seeing the example you set and by hearing the rules you have laid out for them. In addition, if you behave as you'd like your children to behave, they will feel more secure, which will encourage them to follow your example. In other words, if you want a certain behavior from your daughter, modeling this behavior is one way to influence her.

In addition, modeling appropriate behavior will help your daughter begin to establish her own healthy boundaries. More on establishing boundaries will be discussed in chapter 3.

Empathic Listening

When I talk to groups about communication, I often ask them what comes to mind when I say the word *communication*. Invariably the first word that I hear blurted out is *talking*. So many of us consider talking to be synonymous with communicating. And it seems that when we are frustrated and trying to get our point across we continue talking even when no one is listening.

For the first decade or so of your daughter's life you thought talking was your main form of effective communication because you had to keep her out of danger or give her instructions regarding tasks. But as your daughter enters adolescence your style of communicating needs to shift. And this is a perfect time for you to learn about the art and skill of empathic listening.

Seek First to Understand

Any relationship can be improved by following one simple guideline, which defines empathic listening. This is "seek first to understand and then to be understood."[2] Stephen Covey, author of *Seven Habits of Highly Effective People,* uses this phrase throughout his work.

The importance of understanding was illustrated to me when I attended a discussion on dealing with adolescent girls. Both adolescent girls and their parents attended. When parents were asked what they wanted to get out of the discussion, many of the responses had to do with getting their daughters to listen to their advice, or with just getting the daughters to talk to them about their problems so the parents could in turn give them advice.

During the session the girls were very quiet and were never asked a question, so I raised my hand and asked the girls, "What is more important to you, to be understood, or to have someone tell you how you can solve your problems?" Each of the girls agreed that it was more important to them to be listened to and understood than to receive advice. Most said they would probably ask their parents for advice if their parents would simply listen to them for a minute.

Listening to both the parents and the girls in this session, I realized that both the parents and their daughters wanted to be heard. Problems with communication start when we are aware only of our own frame of reference. We may find ourselves ignoring others' feelings or thoughts because we are anxious to solve their problems for them—we are seeking first to be understood, not to understand. This concept is illustrated by a question posed to me by one mom. She asked, "How can I improve communication with my daughter? My daughter often says, 'You do not let me talk.' When she is talking I am not allowed to ask questions. She wants me to wait until she is completely finished talking before I can say anything."

The adolescent girl in the case above just wants to be heard. And feeling as though they have been heard helps build self-esteem in girls. Girls need to feel that they are important, and they feel important when parents really listen to what they say. Thinking that they are important because of the clothes they wear or the friends they have are external sources of reassurance that do little to boost their self-esteem. Feeling heard encourages girls to communicate with their parents and increases their sense of worthiness.

Empathic listening also gives your daughter a feeling of control and empowerment. At this point in her life, she is simultaneously struggling to gain control and is afraid of being in complete control with no one to fall back on. Empathic listening on your part will help your daughter feel that she has the ability to control the outcome of a situation, while having the comfort of knowing that there is someone who will listen to and understand her.

If your daughter has the perception that everyone except for herself is controlling her life, she may become depressed and turn to unhealthy and dangerous ways of gaining a feeling of control, such as overeating, undereating, abusing alcohol or drugs, or engaging in sex. Your listening appropriately may help to prevent problems and enable your daughter to improve her self-esteem.

Of course, listening effectively does not always mean you have to agree with the person you are listening to. Some parents get the impression that listening to their children means that they always have to agree with the child's arguments or solutions. I have had many conversations with young women in which we have ended up agreeing to disagree. These young women may not have been happy about the consequence, but they understood that I cared enough about them to at least hear their point of view.

The Three Components of Empathic Listening

As I mentioned previously, empathic listening involves seeking to understand another person before trying to be understood. In order to truly understand that person's point of view you must actively listen. You are not just sitting back and hearing, nodding your head while you think about your grocery list, but rather you are getting involved in what the other person is saying. Picking up key words, phrases, feelings, and so on helps your daughter to feel loved, supported, and heard.

Empathic listening is made up of three components:

- ❀ paraphrasing
- ❀ validating and reflecting feelings
- ❀ confirming and/or summarizing conversations[3]

Each of these components convey a parent's interest in and support of his or her child. Paraphrasing simply means that, after listening to what your daughter has said, you repeat it back to her in your own words, showing her that you have heard her. Below is an example of paraphrasing.

Daughter   *Hey, Dad, I really want to go to Madeline's party next weekend.*

Dad   *Oh, Madeline is having a party next weekend? (Dad simply repeats back what she is saying.)*

In addition to paraphrasing, try to validate her experience and reflect back what you observe that she is feeling. For example, Dad could say, "Oh, Madeline is having a party next weekend? You sound excited." If you want to be sure that you understand what your daughter is trying to say to you, confirming what you think she is saying would be helpful. You can also summarize the conversation. For example:

Daughter	Yeah, I'm really excited. Everybody is going to be there. Can I go? I know we're supposed to go to Granddad's eightieth birthday party, but **this** party is a-once-in-a lifetime chance to meet **everyone**!
Dad	So let me make sure I'm following you. Madeline is having a party next weekend. This party is on the same day as your grandfather's eightieth birthday party. And you are really excited to go to the party because everyone will be there. Is that right?
Daughter	Yeah, that's right.
Dad	And what do you think your Granddad will say when you call him to tell him you won't be at his party?
Daughter	What do you mean when I call him?
Dad	If you want to miss his party you are going to be the one to tell him.
Daughter	Well, how about I go to Granddad's party, and then maybe you can drop me off at at Madeline's after?
Dad	That seems like a good solution to me.

The Unconscious Reaction

Now that you understand the mechanics of empathic listening, it will be beneficial to discuss a roadblock that often inhibits effective communication: the unconscious reaction. An unconscious reaction is a knee-jerk response to a situation. Essentially, our subconscious mind responds automatically with comments that may be negative or harsh, such as "How can you be so stupid?" or "You are just useless." These comments may sound like those of a parent or another significant person in our past.

When your daughter is exhibiting typical, unpleasant adolescent behavior, something inside of you will want to comment on what she said or how she said it because her comments have triggered some emotion in you, such as anger, frustration, or hurt. Your first reaction is to respond without thinking. It's not something you plan—it just happens.

For example, in the situation previously discussed where the daughter wanted to go to her friend's party instead of her grandfather's birthday celebration the parent might have reacted unconsciously and told the child that she is being selfish and ridiculous. As a result communication would be blocked and not much, if anything, would be accomplished.

The good news is that you can learn to control these comments and even eliminate them when necessary. Becoming aware of your unconscious reactions and learning to anticipate and control them will improve your relationship with your child. Controlling your reaction also allows you to address your daughter's inappropriate comments after the conversation. Discussing these comments when she has calmed down will be more likely to result in your daughter really hearing you instead of becoming angry and stomping off to her room because "you just don't understand."

Obtaining control of your unconscious reaction and ultimately eliminating it takes practice, self-talk, and self-awareness. More about the unconscious reaction and how to handle it will be discussed in the next few chapters.

Building Rapport

Communication experts have stated that only 7 percent of communication involves the actual words we are saying. Roughly 23 percent has to do with our tone of voice, and 70 percent is done through nonverbal methods like matching and mirroring.

When we feel affinity toward someone and our interactions with that person are marked by an unconscious connection (even when we are not actually agreeing with what the other person has said), we have rapport with that person. Rapport is simply a connection that is felt while communicating with another person. It is this connectedness that helps you build a solid relationship with your daughter. To establish rapport with your child during a conversation, you can match or mirror your child's body language, listen for and repeat key words, and respect her point of view.

Matching or Mirroring Your Child

This technique involves subtly reflecting your child's posture during your conversation. People who are sympathetic toward each other often do this unconsciously when they are speaking with each other. When you want to foster rapport and create a connection with your child, you can consciously mirror her posture. For example, if your daughter is sitting with her legs crossed at the ankles you might cross your legs or even your arms. If she is tilting her head a certain way or leaning toward you when she speaks you might do the same while you are talking. When you match or mirror her body language subtly your daughter will not pick up on what you are doing, but she may find herself being more receptive to what you are saying.

Repeating Key Words

Another way to establish rapport with your daughter is to echo key words that she uses when talking with you. When she repeatedly uses a particular phrase, then you can use that same word or phrase when responding to her, conveying the idea that you understand her point of view.

As you know, teenagers often use a unique lingo. And when you use this lingo while talking with them, they will take note of it because they are not used to hearing you use those words. For example, one adolescent girl described her teacher's reaction to a situation as "chucking a psycho." This phrase is probably not in your normal vocabulary, so it would sound foreign to her if you said it. But echoing an off-the-wall phrase can help establish rapport by allowing some humor in the situation. When done occasionally without the intention of ridicule, repeating key words can strengthen your parent-daughter connection.

> One of the complaints I hear most often from teenage girls about communicating with their fathers is that they continue to watch television or read the newspaper while their daughter is trying to talk to them. The most common complaint about mothers is that they don't let them finish what they want to say.

Here is a sample conversation:

Daughter *Agghhh! Mr. Petersen is so rude!*

Parent *Mr. Petersen, your social studies teacher?*

Daughter *Yeah! Him!*

Parent *What specifically has he been rude to you about?*

Daughter *Well, nothing really. He just doesn't listen. I try to tell him that I don't understand something and he just chucks a psycho and leaves the room.*

Parent *He chucks a psycho, does he?*

Daughter *Yeah, his face gets all red and he looks like his eyeballs are gonna burst out of their sockets and then he just starts screaming at everybody.*

Parent *Eyeballs bursting, face getting all red, and screaming. That does sound like chucking a psycho to me.*

Daughter *(Giggling.) That sounds so weird when you say it.*

The situation is defused by the daughter's laughter at the parent's use of her slang phrase. The parent can then steer the conversation toward other methods the daughter might use to approach Mr. Peterson for help.

Respecting Her Position

To communicate effectively means to strive to understand the other person's point of view. Therefore, shooting down your daughter's solution or opinion right away blocks communication. Give her a chance to talk it out or persuade you of the merit of her position. Then, if you still aren't convinced, whenever possible come up with a solution in which you will both benefit. Be careful not to simply play the listening game—do not just pretend to listen, remaining rigid in your opinion. Hear her voice, listen to her feelings and ideas, and remain open to adjusting your position or original plan if appropriate.

For example, a conversation with your fourteen-year-old daughter may go something like this:

◉

Mom	Next month we're taking a family vacation to Hot Springs National Park. It's always so beautiful this time of year.
Daughter	(Groans) Oh, Mom, why do we have to go to a national park? It's going to be so boring!
Mom	So you think it will be **boring**, do you? (Repeating back key word.)
Daughter	Totally boring! Not to mention I have to be in the car with my little brother. He's so annoying. I hate going on family trips. It's torture!
Mom	So what do you think would be a better solution?
Daughter	Well, I could stay at Katie's house. Her parents are totally cool.

Mom	*I understand that you think Katie's parents are totally cool, but I'm not comfortable with you staying there.*
Daughter	*Ahh, I knew you would say that.*
Mom	*Why don't you see if Katie or another friend of yours might like to come along with us? That way maybe you wouldn't have to endure so much torture.*

By paying attention and respecting your daughter's point of view you have accomplished the following:

- ❀ You have practiced your listening skills.
- ❀ You have allowed your daughter to try to come up with a solution of her own.
- ❀ You have understood her belief that she would be bored and does not want to spend time with her younger brother.
- ❀ You have devised a solution that she will be excited about and will keep everyone happier on the trip.

Keep in mind that even after giving her the opportunity to make her case, validating her feelings, and attempting to understand her position, you may have to put your foot down and say, "I am sorry but I do not agree with you and this is why." Do not feel that you have to be her friend and always change your position to accommodate her. Tears and comments like "You never let me go anywhere!" may follow, so be prepared. And although her reaction might be challenging, know that you gave her the opportunity to be heard, you attempted to work with her to come up with a solution that would be acceptable to everyone, and you acknowledged what she was feeling. Even though she was upset, it is important that you stick to your guns when you feel it is necessary to do so.

Here's another example of an exchange that could have been improved by the use of empathic listening. Your fifteen-year-old daughter comes to you, obviously upset:

◉

Daughter	*I really hate my Science teacher!*
Parent	*Now, honey, why would you say something like that? (Blocking communication.)*
Daughter	*Because he's a jerk!*
Parent	*Well, why is he a jerk?*
Daughter	*I don't know. He just is!*
Parent	*OK, give me a reason why you think he is a jerk.*
Daughter	*He gave me seventy on my project! Can you believe it?*
Parent	*Seventy?! You know if you wouldn't spend so much time on the telephone and put some effort into your homework then you wouldn't be getting a seventy on your paper. (Hello, unconscious reaction!)*
Daughter	*(Rolls her eyes and stomps out of the room.) Whatever!*

◉

The daughter was trying to tell her parent something about the science teacher but didn't feel as though her parent was willing to listen. Conversations like these put up communication roadblocks between child and parent. These incidents make the child less likely to want to communicate with her parent.

Let's take a look at how this situation could have been handled more effectively with the use of the empathic listening technique.

◉

Daughter	*I really hate my science teacher!*
Parent	*It sounds like you're really upset with your science teacher. (Paraphrasing and reflecting feeling.)*

Daughter	*Yeah, I am. He's such a jerk!*
Parent	*Boy, you must really be mad to call him a jerk. (Reflecting and validating feeling.)*
Daughter	*Yeah, I am mad. He gave me a seventy on my science project.*
Parent	*(Holding back the unconscious reaction.) So your teacher gave you a seventy on your project. Is that really what's upsetting you? (Paraphrasing, summarizing, confirming.)*
Daughter	*Well, no, it is not just that. I mean I probably deserved a seventy because I didn't put much time into the stupid project. But it is his fault that I hate that class.*
Parent	*(Still holding back that unconscious reaction.) So, let's see, you realized that you deserved a seventy because you didn't put enough effort into the project. And you think all this is due to the fact that you hate your science class and it is his fault. (Summarizing.)*
Daughter	*Yeah, because you should hear the rude comments he makes to some girls in class.*

⊙

OK, now you are getting somewhere. Your daughter came to you feeling upset at her teacher, and because you were able to control your unconscious reaction and really listen, she felt comfortable opening up and telling you the real problem.

Here is another example, a conversation between an eighteen-year-old and her mother.

⊙

Mom	*Are you and what's-his-name going out tonight?*
Daughter	*Mom, I'm sure, can't you call him by his real name?*
Mom	*OK. Sorry. Are you going out with Bill tonight?*
Daughter	*(Hesitating.) Well, yeah. I suppose.*
Mom	*What's wrong? Trouble in paradise?*

Daughter	*You wouldn't understand.*
Mom	*Try me.*
Daughter	*Well, alright, but you have to promise you won't get mad and freak out, OK?*
Mom	*OK, I promise.*
Daughter	*Well, last weekend Bill told me that he is tired of waiting and he wants to have sex. And he said if I don't, that he'd break up with me.*
Mom	*Why, that no-good ___! I never did like him.*
Daughter	*I knew you wouldn't understand. (Stomps out of the room.)*

Now let's look at how this conversation might have gone if the parent had used empathic listening skills.

Mom	*So, are you going out with Bill tonight?*
Daughter	*(Hesitating.) Well, yeah. I guess.*
Mom	*You seem hesitant. Am I right? (Reflecting feeling.)*
Daughter	*Yeah, I guess I am a little hesitant. It's just that we had this conversation last weekend.*
Mom	*A conversation? (Repeating back key word.)*
Daughter	*Yeah. Last weekend he told me that he wanted to have sex and that if I didn't do it with him he'd break up with me.*
Mom	*(Holding back her unconscious reaction.) So, he'd break up with you? You seem worried. (Confirming feeling.)*
Daughter	*No, I'm not worried. I'm just mad. How could he do that to me?*
Mom	*It sounds like you are upset (reflecting feeling) that he would put you in that situation. Do you think if he really loved you he would have had this conversation with you?*
Daughter	*I'm not sure anymore. What should I do?*
Mom	*So, you are unsure about his feelings for you and you are asking for my opinion? (Paraphrasing.)*
Daughter	*Yes. What do you think?*

Mom   *I think you should give this careful consideration and ask yourself whether he would have had this conversation with you if he really cared for you, and think about why you are hesitant. Then I believe you will have your answer. (Using key words, reflecting feeling, giving opinion only after being asked.)*

Some parents have said that they were not sure they would be able to use the communication techniques shown above because it would seem unnatural. As you become better at empathic listening you will adopt your own style, one that feels comfortable to you. Try these techniques on and tailor them to your own personality.

Challenges of Empathic Listening

The most common complaint from parents about empathic listening[4] is that is takes too much time. This process does take some getting used to, and it requires a bit of time at the beginning. Once you have mastered it, though, you will spend far less time worrying about your daughter and fighting with her. Eventually your daughter will, sometimes with your help and sometimes without it, learn how to come up with answers herself. Allowing her to look to herself for answers—with your support and guidance—will help her to have more self-confidence and make better decisions as she grows into a woman.

Lori, a twenty-five-year-old whose parents practiced empathic listening, stated, "I had very little difficulty talking to my parents throughout my teenage years. I always felt they supported me even though many times they did not agree with me. I told my mom almost everything, and some things she probably didn't want to hear."

Another common complaint made by parents about empathic listening is that it seems to give the daughter all the power. True, empathic listening can and will empower your daughter, but it also teaches her how to make her own decisions. If a parent can foster this learning process by utilizing empathic listening, the parent will be more confident in the daughter's decision-making abilities, which she can use and develop as she grows and steps out into the real world. With these benefits, giving up a little power seems worth it in the long run.

Make Time to Talk

One mom writes, "My daughter never picks the right time to discuss things. How do you explain it is not the right time to talk without hurting her feelings?" Although what seems to be a life-and-death situation to your daughter may not seem so urgent to you, understand that at that moment it is really important to her. She has built up the nerve to come and talk to you about what they are feeling. If at all possible, make time to talk.

Catherine Bush, the mother of a fourteen-year-old girl who walked into her Pennsylvania high school and shot another girl in the shoulder, revealed to me one of the things she learned from this horrifying experience. "Never say no if your daughter asks you to go for a walk with her. You never know what she might want to tell you." A few weeks before the shooting, Mrs. Bush did say no to her daughter's invitation to go for a walk because she was tired or busy. "I will never know if going for a walk with her and listening to what she had to say would have made a difference."[5]

When your child wants to talk, put aside what you are doing and listen at least for a few moments. This way you can determine if the matter is something that can wait (her little sister just pulled her hair) or something more urgent. If you absolutely cannot make the time to talk with your daughter at the time she comes to you (if she calls you at work, for example), then make an appointment with her for a time later that day and keep the appointment. The first time you schedule an appointment to talk with your daughter she may be put off or hurt a bit, but as long as you keep your appointment she will learn to trust that you will be there to listen to her.

Stephanie, an eleven-year-old, shared this comment, "My parents are always saying 'Just a minute, we will be right there,' but then they never come back to me to see what I wanted. I always have to go to them and it's just not fair. By that time I am so mad that they forgot about me, I do not want to talk anymore."

One parent had a great suggestion. She felt that she was forever saying, "Just a minute," or "I'll be right there," because she was dealing with younger siblings when her daughter approached her. She noticed that her daughter was becoming more and more irritated with her, even though she did follow through. So this mom started explaining why she couldn't respond right away (for example, "Just a minute, I am changing your sister's diaper").

When I have asked parents who have effective communication with their children how they accomplish this feat, they said that they try to create an atmosphere where their children truly feel they can come talk to them anytime, whether it is three in the afternoon or one in the morning. James, father of two girls states, "Putting our own feelings of 'I'm tired, can't we do this another time?' aside and allowing her to talk shows her that we truly do care."

What If She's Not Talking

You may be thinking, "That listening stuff sounds great, but I can't even get my daughter to talk to me at all. I can't really practice listening if she isn't talking." If so, you are not alone. Parents often comment that their daughters barely speak to them, that if the parent makes an attempt to talk; the conversation usually becomes an argument.

So if all forms of civilized communication with your teen seem to be creating warfare or no response at all, it's time to try some other tactics:

- ❀ Write your daughter a letter.
- ❀ Make eye contact with your daughter.
- ❀ Seek assistance from a counselor when necessary.

Writing a letter, making eye contact, or learning other effective communication techniques will not repair a damaged relationship overnight. Establishing a trusting, supportive relationship takes time for both parent and daughter. When these techniques are applied over time, barriers to communication will gradually break down, making room for healthy connections to grow between parent and child.

Writing a Letter

Letter writing is a common form of communication for adolescents. At school they frequently send notes and write letters to each other. Because it is familiar territory to adolescents, by writing a letter you are, in a sense, entering their world. By writing a letter you can make all of your points without causing a hostile reaction or without getting into an immediate argument. Furthermore, this approach allows your daughter to read your letter at her own pace and to take time to think about what you've written before she responds. The letter can include some or all of the following:

- ❀ Admit that the two of you haven't been getting along lately and that you are willing to take responsibility for your part in the communication problem.
- ❀ Ask to schedule a time when you two can go out for dinner or for an ice cream so you can talk.

- ❧ State that your relationship is a priority to you and that you are willing to truly listen and understand where she is coming from.
- ❧ Promise to refrain from judging her.
- ❧ Promise to listen, and to offer advice only if asked.
- ❧ Tell her that no matter what she may share with you, you will always love her.

Then the hard part—waiting for a response. Give her a day or two to consider what you've written, and then, if she hasn't mentioned anything to you, approach her. When you do, control your unconscious reactions and simply ask to schedule a time to sit down and talk. She will likely accept. If she doesn't respond favorably and you haven't detected any signs warning that something more serious may be going on, then you may want to write her another letter explaining what you want to accomplish. Tell her that you feel you have done a poor job of listening in the past and that you want to start over. After she regains consciousness (she fainted because you admitted you were wrong!) your daughter will most likely give you a chance, because you acknowledged your part in the situation and did not blame her.

At your meeting:

- ❧ Tell her that you would like to put the past behind you and want to start over.
- ❧ Avoid telling her that you are trying to get her to change her behavior. Instead tell her that you are committed to changing your communication style and that you would like her to give you a chance.
- ❧ Proceed slowly and have patience. If she decides to open up, that is great. But do not pry.
- ❧ As difficult as it may be, give up your control; sit back, listen, and apply the skills you have learned in this chapter.

Waiting for an adolescent to respond to a letter can be difficult. If she takes a long time to respond it may not be because she is angry or wants to make you angry. Instead, she may be either fearful of what you will say or do, or unsure of what to say or do. Through the process of letter writing and journaling many young girls become more comfortable and in touch with their thoughts and feelings, so communicating via correspondence can benefit your daughter's development and self-confidence.

Make Eye Contact

Another option is to look your child in the eyes at least once or twice a day. Hold the gaze for just a few seconds but make sure that you communicate with your eye contact that you love her. Parents have noticed an improvement in communication by incorporating this simple yet effective technique. One mother stated, "All I did was make an effort to look at my daughter twice a day for a couple of seconds and think to myself that I love her, and she started talking to me more. It was amazing."

DON'T THINK YOU HAVE TIME TO LISTEN? PARENTS REPORT THE BEST TIMES AND PLACES TO START A CONVERSATION AND LISTEN

Taking a walk

Watching a show together (and discussing it afterward)

Driving in the car

Going to get an ice cream

Right before bed

Writing email to each other

While shopping

Seeking the Help of a Therapist

If you feel you are making no progress in your relationship with your daughter or if she is showing signs of dangerous behavior, it may be time to seek help from a therapist. Family counselors can mediate sessions for you and your daughter. If your daughter is exhibiting signs of a serious problem such as abusing alcohol or drugs, showing suicidal tendencies, or suffering from an eating disorder, a psychologist who specializes in adolescents can help. If your daughter refuses to accompany you, you may wish to attend counseling alone to seek support. Check to ensure that the therapist has experience with adolescents and is educated in adolescent behavior. Referrals from trusted friends, school counselors, or your family doctor are the most common and reliable ways to locate a therapist.

Several studies that examine the connectedness of parents and their children reveal that children who feel they are able to talk to their parents are less likely to practice risky behaviors, including suicide.

Techniques for Communicating and Staying Connected with Your Daughter

Empathic listening and role modeling, discussed in chapter 2, will help you stay connected with your daughter throughout adolescence. This chapter will outline additional tools and techniques that you can use to stay connected with your daughter and guide her through the process of responsible decision making without necessarily telling her what to do. These techniques will enhance your parent-child relationship.

In the conversation below please note the use of paraphrasing, reflecting feelings, summarizing, checking to make sure the parent is understanding the child, and controlling the unconscious reaction. In addition, notice the inclusion of the following techniques:

- ❀ making positive comments
- ❀ asking open questions
- ❀ revealing the parent's own feelings
- ❀ showing the child how she will benefit
- ❀ helping the child come up with her own solution

○

Daughter	You're always telling me to wait! Why do I always have to be the one to wait?
Parent	I can see that you're very upset. Am I right? (Paraphrasing, reflecting feeling, confirming.)
Daughter	Yeah, I'm upset. It seems like you never have time for me.
Parent	You feel I never have time for you? I always come to talk to you as soon as I can after you ask me for something. (Paraphrasing and acknowledging feelings, stating a fact.)
Daughter	Well, yeah, but it's like I am the one who is always pushed away.
Parent	I'm glad that you recognize that I do come to see you as soon as I finish what I'm doing. And I can understand that you often feel pushed away because I'm busy caring for your younger sister. But what do you think are some reasons for my attending to your sister first? (Acknowledging feeling, asking an open question.)
Daughter	Oh, I don't know. Because you like her better.
Parent	I love you and care about you. That's why I'm taking the time to talk about what is bothering you. (Staying calm, holding back the unconscious reaction, revealing your feelings.) Let's try again. What are some reasons that

	would make it important for me to attend to your sister
	first. (Using open question.)
Daughter	*I don't know. Maybe because she is little and needs more*
	help than I do?
Parent	*She may not need my help* **more** *than you do, but her*
	needs at this point in her life tend to be more immediate
	because of her age, just like your needs were at her age.
	Does this make sense? (Validating the daughter's feelings,
	checking to make sure the parent is on the right track.)
Daughter	*I guess.*
Parent	*What do you think we could do to make me available to*
	you sooner? It is important to me that you feel you have
	my attention as well. (Validating the daughter's feelings,
	validating her importance.)
Daughter	*Uh, I don't know. Umm. Maybe I could help with the baby*
	too, sometimes.
Parent	*That's a great suggestion. Sometimes I feel overwhelmed,*
	and I would really appreciate your help. And it would allow
	me to be there for you sooner. We can figure out what
	else you can do in a minute, but now, let's talk about why
	you wanted to see me. (Making a positive comment, reveal-
	ing your feelings, telling the daughter how she can bene-
	fit, and showing that the daughter's needs are important.)

The above conversation may seem idealistic, but if a parent controls his or her unconscious reaction and applies the techniques of empathic listening, the outcome may be similar—the child feels heard and validated and becomes more cooperative as a result. The techniques used above can be applied during any conversation regardless of the topic. In addition, your use of these techniques will help your daughter to develop empathy, self-esteem, and problem-solving skills.

Making Positive Comments

When talking with an adolescent, pointing out positive aspects in the situation and in her behavior makes connecting easier. Adolescents are continually told what they have done wrong by teachers, friends, siblings, and parents. Therefore, pointing out what is positive about their ideas, attitudes, or actions will help bolster their self-esteem if it is done consistently over a period of time.

Psychologist Gabriella Bentley states, "Positive comments are of the highest importance, especially if they are said at random moments," when the adolescent does not expect them.

Some parents worry that they might overdo the positive comments. But as long as the comments are true—"That was a great idea," or "You did a great job"—they will not overinflate her ego. In adolescence she still needs to hear positive comments from significant people in her life because she is unsure of herself at times and hasn't fully developed her self-esteem. This doesn't mean that she should receive only positive comments. For example, if she is doing something hurtful to others, don't be afraid to tell her. Here are some examples of ways to give positive comments to your daughter.

- ❀ "I think you did a great job on that project. How do you feel about it?"

- ❀ "I wanted to let you know that you handled that situation well. How did you feel about it?"

- ❀ At a random moment, put your arm around your daughter and say, "I feel really lucky to have you in my life."

When you need to give your daughter a suggestion or constructive feedback about something she's done, attempt to give her a positive comment first, followed by the constructive feedback: "I know that you get annoyed at your brother for bothering you and most of the time you handle him very well, this time though the way you treated him was inappropriate. How could you have handled this differently?" Or follow the constructive feedback with a statement of support: "I was disappointed with your behavior at school today. I know that you are capable of much better behavior because I see you treat people appropriately at other times. Let's talk about what happened here. I know you can prevent this from happening again."

Asking Open Questions

Open questions are ones that cannot be answered with a simple *yes* or *no*. They begin with words like *how* and *what*.[1] Some examples of open questions are "How could you have handled this differently?" or "What do you think the consequences of your action should be?"

Open questions can, however, result in the dead-end answer so often used by children of all ages, "I don't know." The "I don't know" answer can be a result of a few different scenarios:

- ❀ The child truly doesn't think she knows.
- ❀ The child may know, but doesn't have the skills to express her feelings verbally.
- ❀ The child knows, but is afraid to respond for fear that the parent will become angry or hurt.

Then how do you know whether she is incapable of expressing herself or just doesn't want to respond? Try the following:

- ❀ What does her body language tell you? Are emotions running high? Should you back off until she has calmed down?
- ❀ Simply respond by saying, "I understand that you don't know, but if you did know, what would the answer be?".
- ❀ Reestablish rapport with her by talking to her about something that interests her then revisit the issue later.

❀ Acknowledge her feelings by saying, "It appears that you do not want to talk about this right now, so I am going to respect your privacy and leave you alone. I want you to know that I expect an answer by ___."

What about questions beginning with why? Some therapists suggest avoiding why questions because these questions tend to put people on the defensive.[2] The answers to these questions, if given, are not necessarily true or "why" questions may result in the frustrating "I don't know" answer. As we discussed in the section on open questions, questions beginning with how or what usually result in answers that give the parent more information. For example:

How could you have handled this differently?

What would the consequences be in this case?

What would happen if you did do this?

What would happen if you didn't?

How is this preventing you from ___?

If you have difficulty expressing your feelings in conversation, you can also write your daughter a letter helping her understand what you are thinking and feeling.

Revealing Your Own Feelings

Children who are going through a self-centered phase need to be reminded that what they say can affect another person's feelings. Doing so can help children develop empathy for others.

At times girls would snap at me for no apparent reason (I know—it's hard to believe!). My initial reaction was not to respond. Next I would remove myself from the situation (by either physically removing myself or mentally pausing to maintain composure) before I said anything inflammatory, because that would only give her a chance to escalate the situation into an argument. Taking a break allowed me to collect my thoughts and not let my desire to choke her take over. Joking aside, I would then manage my stress and regain control. A few minutes later, or by the end of my time with her that day, I would approach her and say, "I really didn't appreciate what you said to me earlier. I became angry as a result. I do not treat you that way and therefore I do not expect to be treated that way." In most cases, the girl would apologize either that day or the next day, and then we would sit down and talk about why the situation happened.

By approaching her later when her anger was defused, I was able to regain control of the situation as the adult, and firmly tell her that I reacted with anger because I felt her comments were unwarranted and hurtful. Emphasizing the fact that I do not treat her that way was also effective because it was true. Later, when I would sit down with her and discuss the situation, we would talk about what happened, why it happened, and how she could handle the situation more appropriately next time.

I have often explained to adolescents why I had reacted with anger in order to help them understand their own anger and its source. I would explain that at times my anger was a result of my fear that I might no longer be important to her or that she might not value me. I would tell the girl that behind my feelings of anger was fear, whether it be fear of being rejected, not being taken seriously, not being needed, not being in control, or something else. Having a similar conversation with your daughter after she says something hurtful to you will not only teach her empathy for others but also help her to understand and control her own anger in appropriate and healthy ways.

Some parents have commented to me that they are afraid to reveal their feelings to their daughter because to do so makes them vulnerable. I agree that it makes one vulnerable, but admitting that at times you are vulnerable can enhance your connection with your daughter. Vulnerability is something your adolescent daughter will connect with immediately because she feels that way nearly all the time. Her understanding that you can be vulnerable too, and that you are willing to admit it, can help to foster trust and respect between you and your daughter. You can show your vulnerable feelings at appropriate times as long as your daughter does not become your confidante and witness to all your insecurities. You are not revealing your vulnerability to say, "Poor me," but instead to connect with your daughter and help her understand where you are coming from. Use this technique sparingly and remain in the parental role. You are revealing your feelings to your daughter not as you would to a friend, but instead to create a learning experience for your daughter.

The time *not* to have a conversation about feelings is during an argument or a heated discussion. At these times the person you are arguing with couldn't care less about what other people are feeling because she is overwhelmed by her own feelings. A person who is angry and past the point of regaining control is, in my opinion, simply voicing a desperate plea to be heard. One way to handle this situation is to remove yourself, wait until you have both calmed down, and proceed when you can discuss the subject in a way in which both parties can listen.

Show Your Daughter How She Will Benefit

It is in our nature to do things that benefit ourselves. At first this may sound selfish. But it doesn't have to be selfish. For example, when we help others we may be motivated to do it because it feels good, it is how you were taught to act, or you are committed to helping others as a result of religious beliefs.

We receive some form of payback for everything we do. Life strategist Dr. Phil McGraw asks, "What is the payback you are getting from this action or reaction?"[3] In other words, what is your secondary gain?

Showing or telling your daughter how she will benefit from making a particular choice may help motivate her to act, perhaps even without your having to tell her to do so. One evening a woman named Michele went up to her daughter's room to kiss her good night before bed, a special time between Michele and her daughter when they usually shared a few kisses, cuddles, and kind words. On this night Michele approached her daughter's room and noticed that it was a total mess. She saw that she wouldn't be able to get to her daughter's bedside without stepping on clothes or books. So Michele stood at the doorway of her young teen's room and said, "Sorry, honey. There is so much stuff on your floor that I can't make it to you to kiss you good night. I don't want to step on all your stuff." Her daughter mumbled some surprised response, but her mom blew her a big kiss from the doorway and said, "Good night, I love you," and walked away. The next day her daughter cleaned her room.

Helping Your Child to Come Up with Her Own Solutions

As was discussed in chapter 2, one of the benefits of empathic listening is that you are able to create an atmosphere in which your daughter can learn how to come up with her own solutione to problems.[4] It may even be a solution that failed to occur to you. You allow your daughter to practice making decisions on her own, right in front of you. If you give your daughter opportunities to work out issues in an environment in which she feels supported, she will gain the ability to make decisions effectively when she is away from you. In difficult situations girls often give in to peer pressure because they feel there are no other options. If you guide her to come up with her own solutions in a controlled environment, you may help your daughter see that she has other options besides simply following the crowd.

Below is an example of a conversation that illustrates how this works.

◉

Parent	*I've noticed that you haven't brought Melissa over to the house this week. Is everything alright between you two?*
Daughter	*Yeah, sorta. I'm just not doing as much with her anymore.*
Parent	*Not doing as much with her anymore? You guys were inseparable in the past.*
Daughter	*Yeah, we were close, but not anymore.*
Parent	*Not close anymore? Do you want to talk about it?*
Daughter	*Not really. It's just that she really hurt my feelings last weekend. We were at that party at Gina's, and she knows that I can't stand it when she smokes while I'm around. But she just goes ahead and does it anyway just to look cool. I'm sick of it.*
Parent	*It sounds like you are pretty upset with her. What are you going to do?*
Daughter	*I don't know. I'll probably just ignore her for a while.*
Parent	*Ignore her, huh? Do you think that will get the results you want?*
Daughter	*What? You mean for us to be friends and for her to stop smoking in my face?*
Parent	*Yes, if that's what you want.*
Daughter	*No, probably not. But I don't know what else to do.*
Parent	*Don't know what else to do, hmm. Well, does Melissa know that you are upset?*
Daughter	*I don't know. I haven't said anything to her.*
Parent	*You have known Melissa for a pretty long time. And even*

if she ought to know you are mad, maybe for whatever reason she doesn't know.

Daughter   *So do you think I should talk to her?*

Parent   *Well, that's up to you. Do you know what you want to happen when you talk to her?*

Daughter   *I guess so. I want us to be friends but for her to respect my feelings and stop smoking in my face.*

Parent   *Uh-huh. (Matching or mirroring the daughter's body language.)*

Daughter   *So I guess I should just talk to her and tell her that, huh?*

Parent   *That sounds like a good idea to me.*

More Tips, Tricks, and Techniques

The remainder of this chapter will give parents tips regarding what to keep in mind during conversations and other ways to stay connected with their daughters.

Body Language

When you ask your daughter a question and notice inconsistency between her body language and her verbal answer, you should bring this up to her and let her know that if something is bothering her she can come to you to talk about it. For example, say you have noticed that your daughter seems down or acts depressed and you ask her about it, saying, "Honey, I notice that you aren't yourself lately. Are you alright?" If she responds, "I'm fine!" but avoids eye contact, keeps her head down, and slouches (more than usual), then an incongruency between her verbal response and her nonverbal response (body language) exists. You can reply, "I hear you say that you are fine, but I notice by your actions that you aren't yourself. If you need to talk, I am here to listen." Then, as difficult as it may be, leave her alone to process what you have just said. If you have established good communication in the past, there is a good possibility that she will come to you to talk.

Use of Email

Modern technology can be helpful when you are working to improve communication with your daughter. Kids (and many adults) love getting email. Consider using email to send a letter to your daughter, especially if your daughter checks her email regularly. Keep in mind that it is best to bring your communication back to the face-to-face method eventually.

One working mom of an adolescent girl reported that every day she sends her daughter a short email message. It might be an inspirational quote or just a comment about how lucky she feels to have her daughter in her life. She came up with this idea when she noticed how she felt when she received inspirational notes or stories from friends via email. She said, "If it makes me feel good to receive this stuff from my friends, hopefully it will help my daughter feel good and let her know that I love her."

The Parent-Child Journal

The parent-child journal fosters connection and communication and is most effective when used in conjunction with face-to-face dialogue. The writings that go into it are private and should be seen only by parents and each child. The journal should be kept in a safe place that can be accessed only by the child who writes in it and her parents.

I started using journals when I wanted a tool to help me understand what the girls I mentored and coached were thinking and feeling. I found that, using the journal, I could encourage these girls to set goals and keep track of their progress. I asked them to write questions to me and give me feedback or their opinion, positive or negative, about anything I had done or said. Mostly, I wanted each person to feel important and heard. I was amazed at how much more open and honest the girls were when they wrote in their journal. Some revealed their struggles with eating disorders, self-mutilation, depression, stress, and pain. Others wrote about dreams and revealed goals and aspirations. Once a month I sat down with each girl to discuss these journals and their goals. This process brought us closer together and enabled me to assist some girls who had been suffering in silence.

A parent-child journal can work in much the same way. Each day, every other day, or once per week, your child writes you a message, long or short, about something that is bothering her or something she would like to share with you, whether it be positive or negative. Each time she writes you respond to her entry, asking questions about how she feels or about her goals. Encourage her to share good news as well as bad. Assure her that she will not be judged.

Here are some sample journal entries:

| Parent | *Haven't seen you in a while. Our schedules have been so busy, and it seems like when we are home you're either on the phone or doing homework. Just wanted to let you know I was thinking of you. What's going on with you?* |

Or

| Parent | *You seem a little distant lately. We aren't talking like we used to. Thought we could watch a movie or go shopping this weekend to catch up.* |

Or

| Parent | *I'm concerned about us not communicating. You appear to be a little down. Feel free to write and let me know what I can do for you and how you're feeling.* |

Or

Parent   *Saw your score on your math quiz today. You did a great
job. Keep it up. I love you.*

Make it fun for her. Ask her what she would like to write about. Encourage her to set goals for herself in the different areas of her life. As your daughter becomes more comfortable with writing, you will begin to notice patterns in her thought processes. This may indicate areas where your daughter needs your support or guidance. Completing an entry will often take less than fifteen minutes, or longer if there is a significant issue to discuss. Once a week schedule a time to sit down with each other and talk about any of the entries that warrant further discussion. This meeting should include only the parent and child and may take a few minutes, or more if necessary. These discussions and the parent-child journal provide parents and daughters with a great opportunity to stay connected even during busy times. And it is a great way to show your daughter that you really care about her.

The parent-child journal may introduce your daughter to the concept of journaling. She can find that journaling is an effective way for her to sort out her ideas and feelings and begin her own private journal. If you are thinking, "There is no way I have time to do this technique. I have too many children and/or too little time as it is," know that I used this technique with twelve to fifteen girls at a time. Spending a few minutes a week on each girl resulted in less time spent arguing and wondering what she was thinking and feeling. Because I better understood what the girls were going through, I was able to help them solve problems and feel more positive about themselves.

Parents who have put the parent-child journal to the test have found it to be a great way to stay connected with their daughters. One mom commented, "This journaling is great. My husband and I both do it and it is working really well. As a matter of fact, our daughters have started a journal between each other now."

● ● ●

Handling Stress:
Answers for You and Your Daughter

The first key to handling stress is recognizing the physio-logical signs that go along with it. My personal stress signals are fatigue, tension in my neck and shoulder muscles, and, when I am approaching the point of losing it, shallow breathing. Sometimes if I ignore these signals long enough my face turns red, and I begin to sweat. This is my point of no return. If I allow myself to get to this point, then there is no turning back. I am going to blow.

A situation that could send you to your point of no return could occur after you have had a rough day, for example, and you are just plain tired. The dishwasher repairman never showed up. Your youngest is sick. Everyone is hungry. You had a terrible day at home or at the office. Your daughter walks in and asks you for her volleyball uniform for her game tonight and you realize that you forgot to wash it. The tension mounts and she starts yelling, "I can't believe you didn't wash it! You know I play tonight." Suddenly you are yelling back that she is irresponsible because she could have reminded you or washed it herself or at least put it in the laundry so that when you did a load of wash you would have seen it. Doors are slamming. Both of you are upset. And all this pandemonium is because of a volleyball uniform.

Is it really because of the uniform? No. The uniform is just the catalyst that throws the two of you into a tailspin. The reason for this tumult is not the uniform but poor stress management. We have all been there. What can we do to keep from losing it?

The Fatigue Factor

Fatigue commonly triggers stress.[1] Being tired and worn-out causes people to become irritable, which prompts them to snap at each other or react irrationally. Think back to when your daughter was a toddler throwing temper tantrums. When did they usually occur? Most likely fatigue was often a significant factor. This is true of adults as well as toddlers. We are more likely to lose control when we are exhausted and frazzled.

How do you handle a situation when you are fatigued? What are your stress signals that surface right before you are about to blow? Becoming familiar with your stress signals can help you defuse situations that could cause you to lose control.

When you learn to recognize your stress signals, you'll be able to spot them as they appear, so when a problem like the one with the volleyball uniform comes up you can react more calmly to your daughter instead of snapping at her and creating a big scene. Instead of focusing on something you can't control at the moment (the fact that the uniform is not clean, for example,) focus on what you can control. You might firmly say to your daughter, "Look, instead of wasting our time yelling about something we obviously can't change, let's focus on what we can do about it now." And if your daughter continues to overreact, then simply say, "Look, I am very tired and I refuse to stand here and listen to you yelling. I am willing to help you with the situation. But I will not help though if you continue to act this way."

STRESS SIGNALS

Think of a teapot right before it starts to whistle. The steam has to build up before it blows, doesn't it? Below are some physiological and physical changes that may occur right before you lose your temper.

Tense muscles in the shoulders and neck

Shallow breathing

Increased perspiration

Increased heart rate

Clenched fists

Clenched jaws

Red face

One mom shared the following solution: "When I had a really bad day, I would come home and tell my kids, 'I am tired. I have a headache. I really need you to be respectful and give me some time to myself tonight.'" Sharing her feelings of fatigue worked wonders. She revealed that she was vulnerable and didn't try to hide it. Her children were able to see her as a person who had needs rather than someone they could take for granted.

Defuse It, Don't Lose It

One way to prepare yourself for stressful times is to work on controlling one thing you do an average of 17,280 times per day: Breathing. If you haven't recognized your stress signals and you begin to feel that you are getting irritated or about to lose control, it's not too late. You can still get a handle on the situation and defuse it—by slowing down your breathing.

Diaphragmatic Breathing Exercise

What is diaphragmatic breathing? The diaphragm is a muscle, located underneath the bottom of your rib cage, which divides the chest and abdomen. Relaxation and meditation techniques utilize diaphragmatic breathing to help people become centered and relaxed. Many adults breathe by using the accessory breathing muscles of our neck and chest. Breathing from the upper chest inhibits us from using our full lung capacity, wastes energy, and contributes to feeling tense.

Let's do an exercise.[2]

Lie down on your back, place your right hand on your stomach just below the rib cage, and place your left hand on your upper chest. Now, as you take a deep breath in, notice whether your shoulders are rising, or your stomach is rising under your hand. If you don't feel your stomach rising then you are primarily using your chest to breathe instead of your diaphragm.[2]

Why is this important?

Breathing from the diaphragm is a much more efficient way of breathing that can help you stay centered at times when you feel you are in a potential "blow up" situation. Try it. The next time your coworker or child starts to irritate you, try breathing deeply using your diaphragm. You will notice that you do not become stressed as quickly or as easily. Diaphragmatic breathing will enable you to reverse or stop those initial symptoms of stress. You will be better able to make rational statements and decisions and navigate smoothly through stressful situations.

Visualization

Another effective way to prepare yourself for stressful situations is to decide ahead of time how you will act when confronted with these kinds of difficult times. Pick any past situation in which you lost control. Now picture yourself in that same situation in the future, but envision a positive outcome. Visualize how you and your daughter will look, hear the words that you will say, and feel the feelings you will have after you have succeeded in maintaining your cool. Practice this visualization technique repeatedly over several weeks. This process will help program your mind and your body to handle tense situations successfully.

Controlling Your Unconscious Reaction

The unconscious reaction is the knee-jerk response we have toward people when our buttons are being pushed: "You did what? How could you?" or "How could you be so stupid?" These words seem to fly out before we even have a chance to realize what we were going to say. As we discussed in chapter 2, controlling the unconscious reaction takes practice, self-talk, and self-awareness. Some effective ways to stop the unconscious reaction include becoming aware of your breathing, slowing your breathing, and consciously relaxing your muscles.

Eliminating negative unconscious reactions allows you to stay in control so that your daughter feels it is safe to communicate with you. Even if you feel anxious on the inside when you first start putting these techniques into practice, remember to control your body language and facial expressions while listening to your daughter.

One school counselor with twenty years of experience says she reminds herself to hold back her inappropriate unconscious reactions by placing her fingers over her mouth when she is listening to her students. This reminds her to control her unconscious reaction, enabling her students to communicate freely with her.

Keeping your composure while your daughter is talking will help her feel understood and supported. When she leaves the room you can fall over, throw something, jump up and down, or do whatever you need to do to release your tension.

The Art of Apologizing

You will have times when you aren't conscious of what you are doing or saying, you don't recognize your stress signals, and you just blow your top. We are all human and we all make mistakes. But it's not the mistake that matters. It's what you do after the mistake that counts. You can turn a bad situation into a good one by correcting your mistake and acting as a good role model at the same time.

Simply put, if you blow your top, you should apologize to your child. Some people may believe that apologizing will make them look weak or foolish. However, apologizing, when done sincerely, can be a very effective technique to help you stay connected with your daughter. Think about a situation at work when your boss or coworker blew up at you. How did you feel toward her? Maybe you were angry, frustrated, or upset. But what if soon after the incident your boss or coworker came to you and said, "You know, I am really sorry. I should not have acted that way. I was tired and something else was bothering me. I apologize for taking it out on you." Then how would you feel about this person? If you felt she was sincere and hadn't repeatedly apologized for doing the same thing, you would probably respect her for coming to you and admitting that she hadn't handled the situation correctly. Her apology, if sincere, would lessen your anger toward her. Note that she did not say she was wrong about what she said; she just admitted she was wrong about how she handled the situation.

Apologizing can come in very handy following an altercation with your daughter. After you have both cooled off, if you go back to her and let her know that you are sorry for acting the way you did and that the way you handled the situation was not appropriate, you will reconnect the lines of effective communication. In addition, you should explain to your daughter how you could have handled the situation more appropriately. Don't let her off the hook, though. Ask her to tell you what she thinks she can do to avoid this kind of incident in the future. If you have admitted first that you could have behaved differently, she will be more likely to admit that she should have behaved differently as well.

> Caution: Using this technique of apologizing too often can be hazardous. If you lose your cool too often, your daughter will not take your apologies seriously.

One of the girls I worked with wrote in her journal after I apologized for speaking to her inappropriately, "Thanks for showing me that you think I am important enough to apologize to." Apologizing shows your daughter that you value her feelings, eliminates the power struggle between you, and demonstrates to your daughter that no one is perfect. She will surely respect you more and grow to understand the importance of owning up to one's mistakes.

Adolescent Girls and Stress

Children and their parents are experiencing a great deal of stress these days. Unfortunately, not many children are being taught how to decrease their stress. When children do not learn healthy ways to manage stress, they may turn to unhealthy

**ADVICE FROM THE REAL
EXPERTS: PARENTS OF
ADOLESCENT GIRLS GIVE TIPS FOR
REDUCING STRESS WHEN COM-
MUNICATING WITH THEIR DAUGHTERS**

Some fights and disagreements are unavoidable.
Set ground rules for arguments in advance. Remember,
you are doing the best you can.

Keep trying. If your daughter gets frustrated with you, explain
to her either orally or in writing that building a relationship
takes time and you are giving it your best shot.

If you have a setback, just start again.

If you were wrong, admit it.

Have realistic expectations. Start out slowly. It may take some
time for these new ideas to work. Your daughter is an individual,
separate from you. Respect her opinions and thoughts even
if they differ from yours.

You can only change yourself and control your own actions.

Don't take the disagreements personally.

Be aware of your tone of voice and your body language
when communicating with your daughter. If you speak
to her in an accusatory voice, your daughter will hear
only the voice, not the message. Her defenses will be
activated and effective communication will not
take place. Certainly some messages need
to be delivered in a firm way, but never
in a degrading way.

outlets, such as drugs, sex, over- or undereating, self-mutilation, or suicide.

When I noticed this trend, I began to meet with girls once a week in stress workshops. We discussed what was "stressing them out" and how they dealt with these stresses.

Some stressors haven't changed over the years.

COMMON STRESSORS
FOR ADOLESCENTS

Major stressors:

Grades

Too much homework

Getting into college

Friends (trying to fit in; trying to be popular;
trying to see them on weekends)

Boyfriends (having them; not having them;
worrying about being liked by boys)

Drugs (taking them and risking getting in trouble; not taking
them and risking having social problems from peer pressure)

Sex (having it and getting HIV or getting pregnant;
not having it and looking like a prude)

Parents (being nagged about friends, grades, chores)

Looks (not feeling as skinny or pretty as everyone else)

Extracurricular activities (balancing homework and job with
activities such as sports, ballet, or volunteer work)

Minor stressors:

Uncertainty of the girl's future

The environment

Wanting to be married with
children by a certain age

Adolescents have had to deal with alcohol and nicotine for a long time, but now Ecstasy, heroin, and stronger forms of marijuana are available. Children are selling prescription drugs such as Ritalin to their classmates. Cocaine and methamphetamines are present, but weren't as prevalent as other drugs with the girls I surveyed.

Competition to get into good colleges is more intense than ever before. This creates added stress for students preparing for the SAT and other college entrance exams. Many parents feel this stress as well.

In some school systems more homework is being assigned than in the past. And as students spend more time on extracurricular activities, the amount of time children are able to spend doing homework decreases. This does not mean that extracurricular activities are harmful; when appropriately monitored, extracurricular activities can enhance a child's life. But more is not necessarily better.

Sex also causes stress for young women. These days girls are not only faced with the possibility of getting pregnant if they choose to have sex, but also with the possibility of contracting a fatal disease like AIDS. Pressure to have sex, both from their peers and from the culture in general, is powerful, so choosing not to have sex is challenging for girls today.

Adolescent girls in the twenty-first century face many of the same dilemmas girls did many years ago; however, the stresses are more plentiful, and girls are dealing with these issues at a much younger age than their parents did.

How Kids Handle Stress

I asked a group of girls to tell me how they deal with their stress. Here are their answers:

❀ sleep

❀ listen to music and dance

❀ talk on the phone

❀ eat

❀ take a bath

❀ read something non-school-related

❀ go out dancing

- ❀ watch TV or see a movie
- ❀ get a massage
- ❀ take a walk or go for a run
- ❀ smoke, drink, or take other drugs

Some girls reported that they handled their stress by doing the following:

- ❀ binging and purging
- ❀ not eating at all
- ❀ cutting, burning, or hitting themselves

All of the girls' ways of dealing with stress are only temporary fixes. None of these tactics help the girls to face the problem head-on. These adolescents avoid looking at the actual cause of the stress in their lives. Some of the activities mentioned are good ways to reduce stress in the moment, but if the person does not face the situation that causes their stress, then the stress will never go away. In fact, not confronting the problem actually creates more prolonged stress.

Eliminating Unnecessary Stress

Parents can help their child learn to decrease unnecessary stress by teaching her the following stress-management techniques:

- ❀ Look at the situation and discern what you have control over. You can never control another person. You can only control yourself. You can try to influence another person's behavior by changing your own, but you will never change another human being. Figure out what you can change.

- ❀ Set goals. Goals must be specific and include a date by which they will be achieved. For example, a seventeen-year-old who had to work to pay for her private-school tuition set the following goal: "I will talk to my boss and ask if I can work a later shift so that I can get my homework done on time. I will ask him on September 25 at 9:00 A.M."

❀ Rehearse and visualize. For example, "I will tell my boss on September 24 that I have something to run past him. I will ask him if 9:00 A.M. on September 25 would be a convenient time to talk about it. I will also tell my best friend that I am going to do this so I know I can't back out." Then visualize the goal being accomplished. In your mind, picture walking into your boss's office and broaching the topic. Picture the conversation that follows, and how you will feel after you have accomplished your goal.

❀ Take action: Just do it. Discussing the problem and thinking about it are important, but the stress will only be lessened as a result of taking action.

❀ Focus on what you want, not what you don't want. Usually what we focus on is exactly what we end up experiencing.

❀ If your plan doesn't work out, come up with other solutions. In case your first plan doesn't work out, devise another plan that will include other possible solutions to your situation. For example, "My boss did not let me change shifts so I will give two weeks notice and in the meantime look for another job."

Talking about these steps with your daughter and teaching her to apply them to each stressful situation in her life will help her face these situations head-on. When your daughter learns how to solve her problems and reduce her stress, your stress will likely be reduced as well.

◎ ◎ ◎

Taking a Closer Look at Self-Esteem

The development of self-esteem plays a vital role in our lives. Researchers at the Search Institute in Minneapolis, Minnesota (www.search-institute.org), who have surveyed more than one million sixth through twelfth graders since 1989, have identified forty developmental assets youths need in order to become healthy, caring, and responsible adults. High self-esteem is one of the assets identified. Research consistently shows a dip in the self-esteem of preteens and teenagers. This dip in self-esteem affects both males and females.[1] Though both sexes are affected, even the critics of some of these studies have indicated that girls are more likely to score lower in relation to self-esteem than their male counterparts.[2]

Research studies indicate that self-esteem is a crucial factor in preventing and deterring destructive behavior in adolescents. For example, children who have adequate self-esteem are less likely to be promiscuous and less likely to take drugs. Children with inadequate self-esteem are more likely to feel that there is something wrong with them; they do not like themselves, and they may not like others. Individuals with low self-esteem can be the targets of bullies. They may be at risk for difficulties with eating disorders, unhealthy relationships, depression, self-destructive behavior, and suicide. One young teen who displayed the symptoms of anorexia nervosa wrote to me, "I just want to die. I hate myself and my life. Why won't they just let me die?" Ironically, she was a girl people liked to be around because of her sweet disposition and caring attitude. Everyone else seemed to love her, but it seemed that she could not bear to love herself.

Young adolescent girls consistently report more general health problems, recurrent pain symptoms, and negative feelings such as feeling low or lonely.
1997–98 National Institute of Child Health and Human Development, January 31, 2000, International study.

Most people are familiar with the concept of self-esteem and believe that it is important, but few give much thought to exactly what it is. *Self-esteem* is often used interchangeably with other terms such as self-confidence, self-image, ego, and narcissism.

What Is Self-Esteem?

Pediatric psychologist Dr. Brian Mesinger defines self-esteem as "the collection of beliefs and feelings we have about ourselves." Most people agree it is a feeling related to our self-worth as a human being. A person with optimal self-esteem feels that she can cope with any problem. In other words, a person with optimal self-esteem feels basically competent. She believes she is worthy of being loved. She believes she is a worthy human being, but not worth more than another individual. In addition, she expresses a feeling of authority over herself.[3]

Self-esteem constantly evolves within us. The development of self-esteem is a dynamic process throughout life, not a static state.

Some adolescents seem to have optimal self-esteem; however, due to a lack of experience and resources, as well as dependence on external sources of self-assurance, their self-esteem is vulnerable. Actually, adults who have not worked through issues in their own lives and have not grown to see themselves as worthy may be just as vulnerable as a child whose self-esteem is still developing.

The Development of Self-Esteem

When a child is young the significant people in her life are primarily responsible for the development of her sense of self. These people can be parents, grandparents, siblings, or caregivers. Whoever the child spends most of her time with plays a significant role. These pivotal people in a child's life provide external feedback to the child; psychologists and researchers agree that giving your child positive feedback whenever possible sets the building blocks of optimal self-esteem in place. The reverse is also true; degrading comments, put-downs, and other forms of inappropriate negative feedback from significant adults diminish a child's sense of self-worth, since she has not yet learned to give herself internal feedback and depends on others to tell her that she's OK.

As the child matures, she must shift from needing external feedback to receiving internal feedback in order to develop optimal self-esteem. Low self-esteem can result when a child never learns to shift from seeking approval from others to seeking approval from herself or when she does look inward and she finds little to feel good about. Adolescents naturally tend to shift their awareness inward, so the teen years are the perfect time to help them develop an internal mechanism that builds self-worth. This mechanism also prompts us to conduct internal checks to make sure our actions are appropriate for ourselves, others, and the world around us. The process of building a healthy internal feedback mechanism can begin well before adolescence and continue throughout these years.

Figure 5.1 depicts how the shift to an internal feedback system might progress as we grow. A small amount of external feedback remains important after age thirty simply because most adults still enjoy receiving positive comments from significant people in their life, but they should not need to hear these comments in order to feel good about themselves.

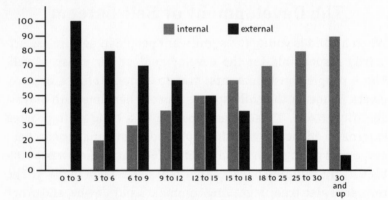

The above graph simply shows that as she develops your child will still need you to stay connected with her and provide some of the external support she needs to develop her self-esteem. Without a strong connection and without positive comments, love, affection, and emotional support from significant people in her life, your daughter will not develop adequate self-esteem and may turn to others who do not have her best interests in mind. Low self-esteem and a need for external approval may lead your daughter to engage in unhealthy risky behaviors, such as promiscuity or using drugs.

You can help your daughter develop a healthy internal feedback mechanism any time she encounters a difficult situation or challenge. Asking your daughter some of the following questions during challenging times will help her to begin the process of developing a healthy internal feedback system.

- ❀ Is this behavior getting you the results that you want?
- ❀ Are you allowing another person to control or determine how you feel about yourself?
- ❀ Have you done your best in this situation?
- ❀ What can you do now to change this situation?
- ❀ What could you do differently in the future to prevent this from happening?
- ❀ What action would you repeat in the future because you were happy with the results?

Internalize Success

Learning to internalize success is part of the development of the internal feedback system. Many girls tend to discount others' positive comments about their accomplishments, saying, "It's no big deal," or "Thanks, but I didn't really do that well." They do this because they don't want to appear conceited to their friends, or because they are uncomfortable receiving positive attention. When you notice your daughter doing this, bring it to her attention and encourage her to be proud of herself when she accomplishes something—in other words, encourage her to internalize her successes.[4]

Parents often say to their children, "I am so proud of you." Unfortunately, this can set our children up to want to accomplish tasks in order to gain external approval. Always seeking external approval can lead to a lifetime of disappointment. Asking her instead if she is proud of herself or how she feels about her accomplishment may result in feelings of self-acceptance and approval. If she answers by saying, "I think I did terrible," or "I am so stupid," you will be able to see that your daughter needs help to learn to evaluate her performance or her feelings in an objective way.

Some girls may feel torn between not wanting to be conceited because no one will like them and allowing themselves to acknowledge their accomplishments and build their self-esteem. If your daughter seems to be torn in this way, explain to her that conceit is the belief that you are worth more than someone else, and that it has nothing to do with allowing yourself to accept your successes and feel good about them. Acknowledging and internalizing her successes is one way your daughter can build optimal self-esteem.

A conversation with your daughter in which you encourage her to own her successes may go something like this:

○

Parent	*By the way, how did you do on that geometry test?*
Daughter	*Fine.*
Parent	*You don't look as if you did fine. How did you do?*
Daughter	*I suck at geometry. I hate that class.*
Parent	*I can see that you're upset about the class. Do you mean you did poorly on the test?*
Daughter	*I told you I'm terrible at geometry. I got an eighty.*
Parent	*(Holding back the unconscious reaction.) It sounds like you don't think that eighty was good enough. Is that right?*
Daughter	*(Rolling her eyes.) Everyone else did better than me. I guess I'm just stupid.*
Parent	*Well, your performance in other classes shows that you aren't stupid. How do you think you could get a better result next time?*
Daughter	*I don't know. Study more, I guess.*

Parent	*Studying more is one possibility. What matters most is that you did your best to prepare yourself for the test. If you didn't, then you can work on better preparing yourself next time. We can talk about how to do this if you aren't sure. And if you feel you did prepare yourself appropriately, then we can discuss what to do next. Let's talk about it after dinner and work it out.*

This dialogue creates options for the adolescent girl. It helps her to see that she can work to control the outcome of a situation, and that her performance does not define who she is. It also gives the parent a feeling of control instead of helplessness. The parent does not react and become angry; he or she makes an attempt to work with the daughter to help her achieve a better result. In the process the parent may find that the daughter needs to improve her method of test preparation, doesn't really understand the material and requires tutoring, or has a problem with the teacher. Gaining this kind of information is more valuable than simply telling your daughter, "Try harder," "It's OK, you'll do better next time," or "I know you are smarter than that." These comments will not help your daughter objectively assess her performance or her feelings about her performance.

Situations may arise when your daughter has performed well but is horrified because she didn't win a soccer game or didn't get 100 percent on a school assignment. A situation like this could be handled in the following way:

Daughter	*Oh, my God, I am so stupid. I can't believe I missed that answer.*
Parent	*You did great, dear. You got 95 percent on the test!*
Daughter	*I didn't do great. I should have done better. I'm such a loser.*

If at this point your daughter is extremely upset, don't keep telling her how great she is or how silly she is being. Either make light of the situation by using humor or just remain calm and wait until she settles down.

Later, when she has calmed down, you can talk with her about the situation:

◉

Parent   Let's talk about what happened today.

Daughter   What? I just got a little upset.

Parent   Yeah, a little upset. What was that all about?

Daughter   I just felt I should have done better.

Parent   Better than what or who?

Daughter   I am just so sick of not doing as good as Mandy. She's always getting the better scores, the higher grades, the cute guys. I am just such a dork.

Parent   It seems as though you are really frustrated because you are comparing yourself to Mandy.

Daughter   Well, I see her every day and she's always better than me no matter how hard I try.

Parent   No matter how hard you try, you will never feel better about yourself or get anywhere in this life if you constantly compare yourself to others. The best you can do is to work hard and make your best effort no matter who is around. Your grades do not determine who you are. You determine who you are by respecting yourself and others. So, tell me, is getting upset and frustrated about Mandy getting you the results that you want?

Daughter   I guess not.

Parent   What specifically could you do to improve your score next time?

Daughter   I don't know.

Parent   OK, you don't know. But if you did know, what would it be?

Daughter	*I guess I could ask the teacher for help.*
Parent	*Great idea! And, if necessary, I know you can come up with other solutions as well.*

Adolescents need someone to guide them to set reasonable expectations as well as help them when the results they get are not what they expected. When significant people in their life consistently take time to help them evaluate their performance in an objective way and evaluate feedback from others, this helps the adolescent girl learn to do it herself in the future. As always, in order to use effective communication, parents must seek first to see the situation from their daughter's point of view and not force their opinions on her. When your daughter learns to internalize her successes and to avoid comparing herself to others she will begin to properly build her internal feedback mechanism.

> Ian Thorpe, Australian swimmer and Olympic gold medalist, has said, "I always judge whether I won or lost a race not by whether I came in first but instead by whether I performed to the best of my ability. This way, I have won every race I have ever been in."

Self-Talk

What adolescents say to themselves repetitively over time also affects their self-esteem. Even more important than what the parents say to the adolescent is what the adolescent says to herself.

Negative self-talk is very common among adolescent girls. Unfortunately, girls often berate themselves by thinking of themselves as "losers," "fat," or "stupid." They may put themselves down or make fun of themselves in order to fit in with their friends, so much so that they begin to believe their negative comments and continue making the same negative comments internally.

These inappropriate negative comments can poison the psyche. Think of the effect carbon monoxide has on our bodies. Just as ongoing exposure to carbon monoxide gradually poisons our bodies, deprives us of oxygen, and eventually leads to our death, so can continuous exposure to negative self-talk be damaging. Though this common practice does not always lead to death directly, constant negative thoughts and beliefs about themselves may lead girls to become depressed, which is the underlying cause of eating disorders, self-mutilation, drug and alcohol abuse, unhealthy relationships, promiscuity, and suicide. At the very least they lower self-esteem and cause girls to believe they can't achieve success.

LAUGH AT YOURSELF

Laughing at yourself about silly things you do is appropriate and helps people to not take life or themselves too seriously. But constantly making jokes or negative comments about yourself to make others laugh is not healthy and can damage your self-esteem.

Most teens do not consider the effects of their negative self-talk—and maybe do not even realize they are engaging in negative self-talk—until you bring it to their attention. Recognizing the unconscious negative comments we say to ourselves takes practice. When teens are aware of the effects these thoughts can have on their mind and body it helps them to stop and become aware of what they are saying to themselves.

Teens can also benefit from understanding that what they say about others is truly an expression of how they see themselves. It is hard for us to see something negative in others unless we have first experienced this trait in ourselves. Repetitive negative comments about others are damaging to our psyche because the subconscious mind interprets these comments as though we are saying them about ourselves.

During a weekend basketball tournament, I became increasingly impatient with a small group of the thirty teenagers I had brought to the tournament. They were talking behind each other's backs and making fun of complete strangers. At one point a girl in the group was making fun of another player who was walking by, making a disparaging comment about the girl's physical appearance. No longer able to contain my anger, I turned to the smug teen and asked, "Do you think you are so perfect that you continue to berate these people you don't even know?" She was obviously surprised by my comment and made no reply. "What about you?" I asked. "How would you like it if someone made fun of the bump on your nose?" She looked horrified, still unable to reply. Her friend replied for her, "Oh, my God," said her friend, "that is the one thing she hates most about herself, her nose." This teen was clearly making fun of other people's appearances because of her insecurity about her own appearance. Her comments about others revealed how she truly felt about herself.

Another point to share with your adolescent daughter is that those who continually boast about their accomplishments usually have low self-esteem. These girls appear as if they feel good about themselves. However, during one-on-one conversations I have had with girls who appear to be overly confident, they have revealed feelings of emptiness and worthlessness. Children who are developing optimal self-esteem are able to talk about their accomplishments in a positive way but do not boast about their success. In addition, they are able to recognize their own role and the contributions of others in their accomplishments.

The following is a conversation a parent might have with her daughter.

◉

Daughter   *Shelly is driving me crazy. She's constantly bragging about how good she is at everything. She brags about her boyfriends, her grades, and her athletic skills. I'm sick of it!*

Parent	So Shelly is driving you crazy, huh? What specifically about her comments is bothering you?
Daughter	I'm just so sick of hearing how much she loves herself.
Parent	Loves herself? Do you really think she loves herself?
Daughter	Well, yeah. Didn't you hear what I told you she said? She obviously loves herself.
Parent	Really? It sounds to me like she feels she needs to say that stuff to impress other people. Do you think she thinks she's worth more than others?
Daughter	Yeah, maybe.
Parent	Well, let me ask you this. In order to believe you are worthy, do you need to believe you are worth more than others?
Daughter	Well, no.
Parent	If loving yourself means you have self-esteem and self-esteem means feeling worthy yourself but not worth more than others, do you think she really loves herself?
Daughter	I'm not sure, but maybe she's trying to convince herself that she feels good about herself and that's why she's saying it out loud all the time.

◎

Helping your adolescent girl become aware of her self talk and helping her learn to control it are imperative. When she realizes that what she says to herself directly affects how she feels about herself, she will gain some control over her self-image.

Differentiating Self-Esteem, Self-Confidence, and Self-Image

In order to illustrate the relationship between self-esteem, self-confidence, and self-image I have used the analogy of a pie. This analogy separates the terms *self-esteem*, *self-confidence*, and *self-image* in order to better examine each term, but keep in mind that these terms are closely related.

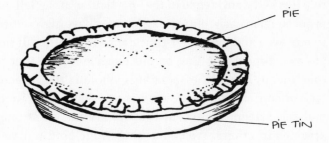

If we take a look at the pie above we see that it has several parts. The first illustration shows the pie tin, which represents the self-esteem of the individual. During adolescence the pie tin can be much more fragile than that of an adult, who has had more experience dealing with difficult situations. The inner being of the individual is the pie tin, which we may not pay attention to or think about, but we trust that it is there adding support.

The illustration below shows the pie divided equally into four parts. These parts represent examples of roles we may play in life. We certainly may have more than four roles that we play in life and these roles may not be balanced as equally as they appear in the illustration, but for simplicity's sake let's look at four equal parts. Your daughter, for example, might play the roles of daughter, friend, student, and athlete.

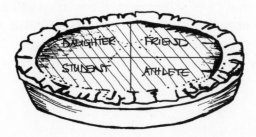

Self-Esteem versus Self-Confidence

Each piece of the pie represents one of our roles. Within that role lies self-confidence in that particular area. Self-confidence is not equal in each role we play. We may have high self-confidence in one area and lower self-confidence in another. It may fluctuate over time depending on our experiences in that particular role. Ideally our self-esteem as a whole is not affected by our lack of confidence in one area or another. When we have optimal self-esteem we accept that we are not as strong in some areas as in others. We can acknowledge both our weaknesses and strengths and address the weaknesses if we choose, or we can comfortably exist with our weaknesses.

Consider Mary, a superb volleyball player but an average golfer. She doesn't mind not being the best at golfing. She is comfortable with the fact that she may not excel at everything. She told me, "As long as I feel I am trying my best and having fun, that is all that matters in the end. I am not going to let the fact that I am not the best at everything take away from who I am."

Unlike self-confidence, self-esteem can be equally distributed throughout all areas of a person's life, and one area does not have to get more self-esteem than other areas. Instead, self-esteem should reinforce or support all the roles we play, or all the different pieces of pie. The pie tin (which represents self-esteem) holds the whole pie and gives equal support to each of its areas. When our self-confidence in one area is shaken, self-esteem, which should be related to our inner being rather than the roles we play, enables us to recover quickly.

The stronger our self-esteem, the less we will allow challenges to our self-confidence to affect our feelings of self-worth. The strength of our self-esteem determines how much or how little damage an adverse situation or outcome will do to our feelings and beliefs about ourselves.

Here is an example that may help illustrate this point. Someone is let go from her job due to downsizing. Her self-confidence may be affected. The person with optimal self-esteem, who generally believes she is a worthwhile, lovable, and capable person, may experience pain, but her feelings of self-worth carry her through and do not allow this situation to shatter her whole being. She goes out and finds a new, possibly better, job. The person with optimal self-esteem looks at the job loss as an opportunity to move on to something better.

Conversely, when a person with low self-esteem loses her job, she may feel, and subsequently act, as though the world has come to an end and her life is over. This person does not bounce back as easily from this challenge. Her self-confidence has been shaken and without adequate self-esteem to support her, she will be less likely to feel confident in establishing a plan and finding a new job. The individual with inadequate self-esteem looks at the loss of her job as yet another sign that she is worthless, and the vicious circle of feeling incompetent continues.

To summarize, self-confidence is a feeling related to how we are doing in a particular role. If we feel we are successful in one area, then our level of self-confidence will be high in that area. On the other hand, if we feel inadequate in one area, our level of self-confidence will be low in that area. Self-confidence fluctuates depending on our experiences. Self-esteem, because it underlies all of the roles we play in life, does not fluctuate with our experiences.

What Is Self-Image?

Our self-image is our internal view of ourselves in a particular role and can be represented by sounds, feelings, and images. Self-image is constantly fluctuating and it relates directly to our self-confidence in that role.

Let's take the role of student to illustrate this point. A person's self-image is how she sees herself as a student. What visual image does she picture in her mind when she thinks of herself as a student? What does she hear in her mind or feel when she thinks of herself as a student? If her grades are good her internal representation of herself will be positive, but if she does not think of herself as a good student the internal pictures, sounds, and feelings associated with her self-image as a student will most likely be negative.

For example, when a girl earns good grades her self-confidence will probably be high in the area of academics, and her self-image will reflect this high self-confidence. But good grades and high self-confidence in one area do not necessarily mean that she feels good about herself.

A woman who attended a small group session regarding mother-daughter relationships supported this point when she told the following story about her ten-year-old daughter. "My husband and I were concerned about our daughter's self-esteem so we decided to do something about it. Her grades were lacking a bit, not failing, but the grades could have been higher. So my husband and I worked diligently with our daughter on her school subjects and hired a tutor as well. Just as we expected, our daughter's grades improved dramatically. Success! Surely now our daughter would feel better about herself. Or so we thought. When I asked our daughter if she felt any better about herself because of her grades, her reply was, 'No.' Of course I was shocked and couldn't believe her answer. She must have noticed the look of disbelief on my face because, without prompting, my little girl replied, 'Mom, I am glad I am doing better in my studies and now I know I can do it, but it didn't make any difference in how much I like myself.'"

The cause of her daughter's low self-esteem obviously lay in an area apart from her role as student. She achieved high self-confidence in this role and her self-image no doubt also improved in this area, but her feelings about herself outside of her role of student did not change.

What Happens When Self-Esteem Is Linked to One Particular Area?

Now let's take a look at the pie below, which represents a typical adolescent girl. As you can see, the role of friend becomes much larger in comparison to the other roles. Notice the role of daughter becomes significantly less, but still exists. The self-esteem of a typical adolescent girl depends very little on the inner being as a whole. Instead, this individual's self-esteem is linked to her role as friend. So when something goes wrong in the friend department, her self-confidence, self-esteem, and self-image will suffer greatly. When she stacks up her worthiness in one area, and problems occur that she does not know how to handle, her world may seem to come crashing down on her, resulting in feelings of low self-worth. Her friends, the significant people in her life who had helped build her self-esteem, have turned on her. If she links her worth as a human being solely to her role as friend, she will find little solace in her other roles.

Linking self-esteem or self-worth solely to one aspect of life can result in low self-esteem in an individual when that particular area of her life is not going well.

Friend "Shifts" and Self-Esteem

Amanda is a fifth grader who has many friends at school. All of a sudden the girls who last week were her best friends aren't talking to her and are excluding her from activities. Amanda seemed to have optimal self-esteem and self-confidence before, but now she is acting withdrawn and is extremely upset about this situation.

Amanda had linked her self-worth to the acceptance of her friends. She had linked her self-esteem to the more fragile and ever-changing self-confidence in this particular role. When she experienced problems in this area that she had never experienced before, her self-confidence and self-esteem were shaken. She felt she was not listened to or respected by her friends, and therefore she began to believe that she was not important. In addition, she hadn't developed healthy and affirming mechanisms for dealing with this pain. As a result, her self-esteem, self-confidence, and self-image were damaged. This experience is common among adolescent girls and provides a great opportunity for parents to guide their daughter to begin looking inside herself for her worth rather than relying on other people to build her self-esteem. Using effective communication skills and working out a plan with your daughter for how she will handle this situation will help her get through the crisis and increase her self-esteem in the long run.[5]

Relationship Trauma

Another common situation occurs when a young woman defines her self-worth through a romantic relationship. For example, Sarah based her self-worth solely on one external entity, her boyfriend. In this situation, while she had a boyfriend and he liked her, her self-confidence grew. When asked how she felt about herself, Sarah would reply, "Great. I feel good about myself," as long as her relationship with her boyfriend was going smoothly. A few months later Sarah's boyfriend broke up with her and she was devastated. Her self-esteem came solely from being loved by someone else. She felt she needed someone else to complete her, and Sarah took her boyfriend's leaving as an indication that she was not lovable. The boyfriend left, and her self-confidence and self-esteem went with him.

These painful situations are common in adolescence and may affect a girl's capacity to feel loved or worthy. A young girl whose self-esteem is linked to something external such as a boyfriend will be likely to say or feel, "He was all that I had. When I was with him, I felt good about myself. Now that he is gone I have nothing." Although this experience is painful, it offers another great opportunity for a parent to encourage her daughter to examine the sources of her self-esteem. She can begin to understand the importance of not basing her feelings about herself solely on one role in her life. She can also learn that attaching your self-worth to something external, such as the thoughts or opinions of another person, sets her up for horrible pain.

Michelle, a fifteen-year-old, once said to me, "It never even crossed my mind that my boyfriend and I breaking up may not be related to who I am as a person. I was depressed for months. I thought it had to be my fault. Somehow I wasn't good enough. But now I realize that both of us caused the breakup. He had difficulty with relationships and I just wanted so much to be the center of his life that it was too much to handle. I guess I just lost myself in him."

Stress the importance of loving yourself first. Instead of looking for someone to "complete" her or make her life better, a girl should look for someone who will complement her life. The adolescent girl can learn at this stage that she, not her boyfriend, is responsible for improving her life.

Getting Caught Up in Her Pain

It is common for parents to experience sadness when their daughter suffers. But getting caught up in the pain their daughter is experiencing does not help her to find the answers she needs in order to move on from the situation. Some parents can't bear to see their daughter go through difficult times. They reveal that they get so upset or angry when their daughter shares negative experiences with them that they cry or have to leave the room. Often both the daughter and the parent play the victim role, thinking "Poor me," "It's someone else's fault," or "How could this happen to me (or my daughter)?" This attitude hinders rather than reinforces the development of healthy coping mechanisms, such as saying, "Alright, this happened. So what am I going to do about it?"

Instead of compounding your daughter's suffering by adding in your own, introduce her to the concept of self-authority, which will strengthen her self-esteem. Encourage her to find ways to solve the problem and play an active part in making her own happiness. One mom revealed her struggle with this issue when she wrote, "My husband says that we just have to help our daughter deal with it. But I get so angry and upset when I see her hurting so deeply that I can't just 'deal with it.'"

The importance of not getting caught up in a girl's pain became evident to me when I asked one adolescent girl why she chose to talk with me instead of with her parents or her friends. She replied, "Because you don't get all upset or act like you feel sorry for me. I know you care because I can see it in your eyes. I like talking out my problems with you because you help me think of ways out of the problem instead of getting all emotional and stuff."

When you feel yourself getting pulled into your daughter's pain, step back from the situation and try to see what guidance she needs right then. Your daughter's self-esteem will strengthen if she receives proper guidance regarding how to handle challenges. Without guidance, she may avoid dealing with challenges. With too much guidance—if you are overprotective and continually attempt to solve her problems for her—she will not gain authority over herself and she will begin to believe she is incapable of handling difficult situations.

Adolescents, just like adults, will go through trying times. Parents who have guided their daughters to solve their own problems and have only intervened when absolutely necessary have reported that they believe their daughters are capable of handling the many ups and downs of life.

Pain Is Inevitable, Suffering Is Optional

Most adolescent girls will experience pain and have to grieve a loss or disappointment at some time. Grieving is a healthy and normal process. Let her experience her pain and face her feelings. Pain is an inevitable part of life, but if we allow ourselves to feel our pain and go through the grieving process, we can avoid excessive suffering.[6] Teach your children how to experience their pain, limit their suffering, recognize their role in the situation, and move on in life.

Instead of saying, "Oh, it's OK. You will get over this," acknowledge her feelings and then give her guidance. For example, a parent could say, "I see that you are hurting right now and this has been difficult for you. When you face these feelings and acknowledge them, you will be able to let them go and move on. Ask yourself what you can learn from this situation and how you can seek the results you want."

Self-Esteem Issues May Be Difficult to Spot

In some girls, low self-esteem may be difficult to recognize if in most aspects of their lives the girls appear to be happy. Suppose your seemingly perfect daughter suddenly faces difficult news: perhaps she is a dancer and has damaged her knee, interrupting her dancing career. If her world falls apart and she does not show signs of overcoming this dilemma, her reaction may indicate there is a self-esteem problem. But if she had adequate self-esteem, then although she would still experience pain and grief, she would eventually be able to recover with a realistic attitude. With effective support from her parents, peers, and mentors, she would gradually regain a positive out-look on life.

Her overreaction and inability to regain her confidence may indicate that dancing was the one area of her life that pro-vided her with a feeling of adequacy. Now she feels she has nothing to fill the gap. She may say things like "Dancing was all I had," or "That was the only thing that made me feel good about myself." She has linked her self-confidence in one area of her life to her self-worth overall.

Her parents, other significant adults, peers, and possibly a therapist or counselor can help this young woman reevaluate her perspective and learn a very valuable lesson. She will be able to take a look at her life and recognize other areas in which she excels and learn to distribute her self-worth more equally throughout the many areas of her life.

Below are some suggestions to help your daughter see the bigger picture.

- ❊ Ask your daughter to identify and write down the vari-ous areas or roles she plays in her life. Discuss those areas when she feels comfortable.

- ❊ Ask her to write down the positive aspects of her life.

- ❊ Ask her to write down areas in which she could improve.

- ❊ Ask her to write down what she can do to improve in those areas.

- ❊ Assist her to write down goals for each of her roles in life for the next three months, six months, one year, and three years.

A parent can help prevent self-esteem issues from sneak-ing up on her apparently confident daughter by paying atten-tion to her self-deprecating comments and by periodically asking her how she feels about herself. Talking with her about all of the areas in her life may give a parent an indication of any potential problems.

Is Your Daughter Suffering?

Girls often experience difficult situations that their parents know nothing about because they happen at school or between friends. Since on the surface things seem to be fine, parents may not realize what is going on inside their adolescent's mind. It is not uncommon for parents of youths who have gotten into trouble to say, "He seemed fine," or "I didn't know she was hurting. She has lots of friends and does well in school." You can never be absolutely sure your daughter has optimum self-esteem, but you can maintain a connection that will help you notice when she is struggling and needs your assistance.

Make a habit of asking your daughter key questions as she travels through adolescence. The immediate answers to the questions are not as important as the process of getting your daughter to think. Over ice cream, at bedtime, or in your parent-child journal, ask your daughter the following questions, which may shed some light on the development of her self-worth:

❀ What parts of your life seem to make you the happiest?

❀ Are you happy only when these areas of your life are going well?

❀ If something happened and these areas of your life were taken away, how would you feel about yourself then?

❀ Do you feel you could go on and live a happy life if these parts of your life were gone?

❀ Do you think you would still like yourself?

❀ What do you like about yourself?

❀ Do you feel like you are in charge of your life or does life just happen to you?

❀ What about yourself or your life needs improvement?

One young woman said, "If my mom asked me these questions all at once I would tell her to bug off!" Clearly, your daughter will be more receptive if you wait for appropriate opportunities and ask just one or two of the questions at a time. These opportunities will present themselves at times when tension is low and just the two of you are present. You'll get better results if you ask these questions in your parent-child journal or during a friendly conversation than during a confrontation.

One mom of an older adolescent girls commented, "I try to use these questions when there is something in the news, on a television show, or happening in my daughter's life that either my daughter brings up or I notice is going on. When I do this, my daughter doesn't feel as though she is being interrogated. But I can tell it gets her thinking."

When you ask your daughter one of these questions, you may not receive a reply. As a matter of fact, if you do receive a reply it might be something like, "Mom (or Dad), you are so weird." (Take this as a compliment. You are supposed to seem weird to your teenager if you are a parent.) If your child does respond, listen for subtle attempts to send you a message. A statement such as "Something seems to be missing from my life" or "I hate the way I look" may be an indicator that your child needs guidance from you. Utilizing the effective communication techniques you learned in the previous chapters will help you assist your daughter in sorting out her thoughts. Consider the following conversation.

◉

Daughter	*Ugghh! I'm so fat. Look at this roll of fat on my stomach. It's so disgusting. (Daughter is sitting down and slouching forward as she pinches excess skin around her middle that flattens out when she stands up.)*
Parent	*You think you're fat.*

Daughter	*Well, look at this. Can you believe it?*
Parent	*Actually, yes, I can believe it. That's called your skin. When you stand up you'll see that it goes away.*
Daughter	*It's still disgusting. I hate my body.*
Parent	*You hate your body? What are you comparing it to?*
Daughter	*Well, you should see this girl at our school. She is so skinny and has really big boobs and all the guys look at her.*
Parent	*Which guys specifically are looking at her?*
Daughter	*All the guys but especially those nerds Jim and Danny. They practically drool all over the place when she walks by. They're so creepy.*
Parent	*Do you wish Jim and Danny looked at you in that way?*
Daughter	*Oh, please, that's disgusting. Get real!*

The above is a real conversation between an adolescent girl and an adult. By remaining calm and refraining from saying, "Oh, stop it. You are not fat," the parent gains a glimpse into her daughter's life. She is finding out information about what and whom her daughter is comparing herself to, and about her ambivalence regarding boys. This information can be tucked away and brought up again at another time, when the daughter is ready to talk about these issues.

What Role Does Body Image Play?

Our body image is our internal representation of our physical body. This image, sometimes an accurate depiction of our bodies, sometimes not, results from comparing our body to other bodies that we think look good. Body image plays a significant role in an adolescent girl's life and can directly affect a girl's self-esteem into adulthood.

Our society has accepted a media-generated version of the ideal body. Poor body image affects self-worth and self-esteem because in our culture external appearance is linked to a person's worth. When girls feel that they do not live up to the standard of the ideal body, then they feel less worthy—unless they understand that what they see in magazines and on television is not the real thing.

Factors That Influence Body Image

Adolescent girls worry about their bodies. A young woman may place an unhealthy emphasis on her body image due to many different factors. A young girl may be excluded from a group at school because the other girls say that she is fat or doesn't wear the right clothes. Or she may be labeled as fat by a sibling or other relative at home. As a result, she receives the message that she is not worthwhile because of her appearance.

What she hears from significant individuals at home may distort her body image. If her mom or her sisters are continually talking about how fat they are, the young girl will internalize these comments. For example, a client of mine talked to me about how she couldn't believe that at the age of seven her daughter was already saying that she was fat and that her stomach was too big. It wasn't such a shock to me, because every time I saw this client she complained about how overweight she was and how she couldn't stand her stomach. The daughter was obviously picking up on what her mom was saying at home.

Countering the Media's Role

Consider the effects of the media-generated perfect body. On television and in movies the typical female is thin and often passive, dependent, valued for her looks, and always looking for a man to complete her life. And the size of her chest indicates that the Breast Fairy must really work overtime! The perfect female body, so prevalent in movies, television shows, and magazines, is impossible for most women to attain. And yet women and especially girls strive to make their bodies match those they see on television and in movies—a losing battle.

Parents must become conscious of the media's powerful influence on their daughter's body image and discuss this with their daughter. Let her know that the images she sees are not real because by the time the pictures of their favorite model appear in a magazine they have been airbrushed, digitally altered, and touched up so no flaws can be seen. Tell her that less than 10 percent of the world's population have the physical characteristics of a supermodel.[7] Discuss the difference between being healthy and being too thin. Help her to become aware of the normal body changes that occur during puberty, like weight gain, breast development, growth spurts, and widening of the hips.

Joe Kelly, executive director of Dads and Daughters (www.dadsanddaughters.org) and father of twin girls, talks about his role in combating the messages from the media. "If I am there countering those messages obviously at home, if I am interested in what she's thinking, who her friends are, talking about my work, being involved, treating the women she loves with respect—I'm sending these powerful messages to her that it's what is inside that counts and that the culture is wrong."[8] Girls need their parents to counteract the media's messages during adolescence because their body image fluctuates throughout this period of time.

Become conscious of what you say about your own body, and eliminate any derogatory remarks.

Talk to your daughter about her idea of an attractive body, and look through one of her magazines together. After you give her a chance to share her views, you can tell her how technology is used to make models look perfect in magazine ads.

Share with her that no matter what she does she is unlikely to look like the women she sees on television because the appearance of those bodies has been altered by computers, lighting, and sometimes even body doubles. Emphasize that she is attractive and can strive to be healthy, and that she will look her best when she is healthy.

SUGGESTIONS TO HELP YOUR DAUGHTER

Gather up a bunch of old magazines. Ask her to cut out pictures of body parts that match how she thinks her body parts look. Have her make a collage. Then have her make a collage using pictures that depict how she would like to look. Sit down together and talk about this. Listen to her and do not tell her that she is wrong; just give her your feedback. Suggest that she get feedback from other people she can trust.

Refrain from describing others as fat or skinny. Talk about their positive characteristics that make them a good person instead.

Give occasional positive comments about your daughter's physical attributes.

Compliment her on aspects of her appearance that she is not trying to change—her eyes or her skin. Don't mention how she's lost weight or reduced the size of her waist.

Dads can have a
great impact here. Whenever
you compliment your daughter on
her physical appearance, also mention
that who she is inside is more important than
how she looks. Subtle comments like this, made
occasionally but consistently, go a long way toward
improving body image and boosting self-esteem.

Frequently remind your daughter that she comprises many
parts and plays many roles. Encourage her to not overemphasize
any one of those areas (e.g., body image, student, daughter,
friend) and to try to keep a healthy balance.

Do not *ever* demean or tease your daughter about her appearance.

REALIZE A HEALTHY BODY IMAGE

If she is wearing makeup and it bothers you, first ask her why she
thinks she needs to wear makeup. Listen to her, then share your
feelings. Tell her that you do not feel she needs to wear makeup
because she is naturally beautiful. This comment made by her
dad can be valuable. If you find yourself berating your daughter
over her appearance, you should examine why you are acting
this way. Are your own insecurities prompting you to make
such remarks? Are you afraid she is growing up too fast?

Let your daughter hear you say something nice about
her character to someone else. An example of such a
comment is, "Yes, she is beautiful, but what I am
most proud of is the wonderful person she
has become."

Building Your Daughter's Self-Esteem

Differentiating self-esteem from self-confidence and self-image is useful, but what else can parents do to steer their daughter toward developing optimal self-esteem?

What a Parent Can Do

In addition to guiding your daughter through the process of shifting the root of her self-esteem from an external source to an internal one, you can foster her self-esteem in many ways. The following chapter lists twenty ways in which you can help build your daughter's self-esteem.

#1 Give Her Unconditional Love and Acceptance

Does your daughter feel that you will love her unconditionally no matter what she does? All parents want their child to feel loved. Granted, you may not agree with her and at times you may even impose consequences for her undesirable behavior, but it is still possible to love her unconditionally. If you disapprove of something she has done, let her know that you are disappointed or angry because of her actions, and you still love her. Tell her that she will have to face the consequences of her actions. You can tell her how you are feeling as a result of her behavior, whether it be angry, disappointed, frustrated, or all of the above. Help her to understand that these feelings are directed at what she did, not who she is. Communicate that you know she can make a better decision next time and remind her that even though you disapprove of what she did, you still love her; this will help her believe that you still have confidence in her and that you love her unconditionally.

One father of four adolescent girls remarked, "When I feel that it is appropriate for one of my daughters to deal with a consequence secondary to her negative behavior, I always follow up my explanation of what the consequence will be by telling her that I truly believe she is a good person and that the behavior that she has shown is not consistent with how I have observed her in the past. What this does is allow me to ask her if everything is going alright or if she needs to talk to her mom or me about something that she may be struggling with. Most times, it is just an isolated incident, but every once in a while they want to talk. And that's when I just sit back and listen."

Trina's Story

Trina, sixteen, told the following story. "A bunch of us got caught for drinking at a party. Somebody called school and we each had to meet with the director of athletics because we were all involved in sports. My mom went with me to the meeting and she agreed with the director of athletics that I should have to face whatever consequences were necessary. I was really mad at my mom for that because some of the other girls' parents were sticking up for them, saying the punishment was too hard or even denying that their daughters drank to try to keep them out of trouble.

"When we came home from our meeting I wouldn't even talk to my mom. I was so mad because she just didn't listen to me. We started yelling at each other and she wouldn't let me tell my side of the story. We ignored each other for a few days and then all of a sudden she asked me to talk. She said that even though she was angry with me for doing what I did and felt I deserved to face the consequences, she said she wanted to hear my side of the story. After I finished telling her my side, she didn't change her mind but I felt much better because she actually listened to what I had to say. She also told me that, even though I made a poor choice, she still loved me. That comment didn't make me like facing the consequences, but it did seem to take away my anger."

It meant a great deal to Trina that her mom made the effort to listen to her side of the story. Trina felt bad for having disappointed her mom, but hearing her mom say that she still loved her kept the door open for future communication and allowed Trina to accept her mom's unconditional love.

#2 Respect Her

When you respect your daughter, she is more likely to respect you. By allowing her privacy and listening to her opinions you will show your daughter that you respect her feelings.

Allow Her Privacy

As your daughter enters adolescence and her body begins to change she will stop running around the house after her bath or she will lock the door when she is in the bathroom. She will begin to need privacy.

One ten-year-old girl wrote, "My brother and sisters are driving me crazy. They won't leave me alone. I have to do my homework and they are right there. I am taking a shower and they always barge in or bang on the door. Dad doesn't understand why I am angry but I just want to have some time to myself. Help!"

According to the mothers I interviewed, all it takes to decrease this tension in the family is to communicate to the siblings that there are certain times when they must leave their sister alone, and to talk to the girl's father about the importance of privacy to his growing daughter. One mother of a twelve-year-old suggested that parents should talk to their daughter about the necessity of spending appropriate amounts of time in the bathroom so that the daughter doesn't "hog" the bathroom and allows other family members to use it when they need to. Emphasize to your daughter that if she wants her privacy you will help enforce this, and she must do her part in the bargain by spending a reasonable amount of time in the bathroom.

Snooping

Snooping is a common way that parents invade their daughter's privacy. However, adolescent girls do not seem to be bothered by their parents' occasional checks of their rooms when they are not home. If a parent frequently rifled a girl's belongings, though, she would certainly begin to feel invaded.

Girls tell me (and I agree) that reading any personal diary is absolutely forbidden. If you have a healthy connection with your daughter and pay attention to your relationship and her needs, you'll pick up signs if something is wrong. Going through her diary should not be necessary except in extreme circumstances.

Eliminate the need to snoop by maintaining a parent-child journal (see chapter 3), which will help you stay connected and up-to-date on your daughter's thoughts and concerns.

When She Shuts You Out by Shutting the Door

Difficulty with respecting your daughter's privacy may arise when your daughter suddenly begins to shut you out. The bedroom door closes and she talks on the phone to her friends instead of to you. Moms confess that this behavior results in feelings of sadness and insignificance in them. Remind yourself that this is common adolescent behavior; it does not mean that you are insignificant, but instead that she is a typical adolescent girl.

Remember that at this point your daughter will probably stop telling you quite as much about her thoughts, ideas, friends, and activities. Look for situations in which you can encourage communication and connection with her and do not expect her to tell you everything. After all, you don't tell her everything, do you?

She Says It's Black; You Say It's White

Respect your daughter's opinions. Listen to what she has to say. Be honest about whether you agree or disagree and let her know that sometimes it is perfectly fine to disagree. If she argues about certain household rules, explain your reasons for the rules. You may be inclined to say, "Because I said so," or "This is my house and I make the rules," but making these kinds of statements will discourage communication. If you explain your reasoning at least your daughter will understand that you are not against her, as long as the same rules apply to everyone in the house. She will probably still be unhappy about the rules, but since everyone has to adhere to them she will know you are being fair.

During adolescence, girls are trying to liberate themselves from their parents, so your daughter may reflexively argue with you even if she actually agrees with you. If she argues all the time and behaves inappropriately, explain that her behavior is not acceptable. Ask her how she would feel if she were treated in the same way.

Behavior Modeling Revisited

Model respectful behavior for your daughter. If you are disrespectful to her, to yourself, to your spouse, to your friends, or to the person calling on the phone just as you are sitting down for dinner, should you be surprised if your daughter picks up this habit and models it back to you? Chances are that if your daughter is not showing you respect, respect has not been shown to her.

If you believe that you model respect but that her peers' disrespectful attitudes are rubbing off on her, say firmly with intense eye contact, "I never treat you that way, and I do not appreciate being treated like that." Or say, "I do my best to treat you with respect. And therefore I expect the same from you." Whenever a girl has spoken to me disrespectfully I have always followed up with her after both of us have calmed down, and talked about what happened and how it could be prevented in the future. Every time I have done this, the young girl has apologized and given me an explanation for her behavior. Each time the outburst has had nothing to do with me; instead, she was upset or irritated at someone else or about another situation. I just happened to be the "lucky one" who was on the receiving end of her frustration and stress.

#3 Model and Enforce Boundaries

One of the most important parental tasks is to establish and enforce boundaries. Parents need to set certain boundaries or limitations in order to teach children what is acceptable and what is unacceptable behavior. Some boundaries are established in order to ensure the safety of children. Depending on the situation, these boundaries or limitations may change as the children age. And the older the child is, the more explanation she will usually need about why particular boundaries are set. Researchers have noted that parents who set limits that are age appropriate and based on logical and natural consequences and who demonstrate warmth and nurturing are most likely to promote optimal self-esteem in their children.[1]

Modeling appropriate personal boundaries and behavior in regard to how we allow others to treat us is also essential. Creating and enforcing our own personal boundaries teaches our children to do the same. If we allow people to take advantage of us, then our children will pick up on this and not learn how to set personal boundaries for themselves. Adolescent girls who have difficulty with peer relationships often lack these personal boundaries. If they do not verbally or nonverbally show their girlfriends and/or boyfriends that they will not tolerate being treated poorly, they may be taken advantage of. Having unclear boundaries or no boundaries can lead to problems with self-esteem as well as self-destructive behavior.

Without boundaries a person's weaknesses or insecurities are out there for everyone to see and exploit. An eleven-year-old girl said to me once, "It was like I was under her (a bully's) spell. She knew just what bothered me and I couldn't or wouldn't stop her and I don't know why." The bully apparently sensed this young girl's vulnerability and made her a target. When approached by the bully, the young girl did not know how to enforce her personal boundaries and prevent the bully's "spell." However, this eleven-year-old received ongoing support from her mom, which allowed her to learn how to handle the bully on her own. This decreased the bully's hold on her and she was able to make other friends who treated her appropriately. When I asked her what she learned from this situation, the young girl replied, "Well, I learned that I cannot let people treat me like that. I have to tell her to stop or she will be in trouble."

One sixteen-year-old I worked with continually let her friends take advantage of her. She revealed to me that she felt "like a

Parents who fail to set their own personal boundaries by allowing other people to take advantage of them or treat them inappropriately are modeling these behaviors for their daughters. Without being consciously aware of it, their daughters may pick up these behaviors and fail to set appropriate boundaries for themselves. Practicing how to handle confrontations before they happen is one technique that a mother of three grown daughters says, "can't be emphasized enough. Doing this," she says, "helps girls enforce their boundaries when they are in a situation and they feel more confident about how to act or what to do."

doormat." Her heart felt trampled; she felt powerless and didn't know what to do. All she wanted was to be accepted and loved. She did not enforce any boundaries with her girlfriends. She allowed them to misuse her, in hopes that she would be loved.

Work with your daughter to help her establish appropriate boundaries. Once she realizes that she can control situations by changing her body language and her internal dialogue or self-talk, she will notice that her reaction changes and she will begin to feel better about herself.

#4 Work on Your Own Self-Esteem

When parents demonstrate the characteristics of optimal self-esteem, their children pick up this behavior and tend to rate themselves higher in the self-esteem category. Parents who exhibit low self-esteem tend to model this for their children as well. In the surveys I conducted with over two hundred adolescent girls, their rating of self-esteem tended to be similar to how their mothers rated their own self-esteem. That is, their perception of their mom's self-esteem was closely related to their own self-esteem.

Ask yourself how you rate your self-worth. If you have low self-esteem you will convey this message to your child. If she hears you saying, "I am stupid," or "I am fat," or "I can't do that," your child is likely to internalize those negative comments and begin to feel the same way about herself. Even if you do not make these comments but your actions show that you have low self-esteem (for example, you do not enforce your personal boundaries), your daughter will pick up on this as well.

When your child is young, you are her world, her main source of information. Send her positive messages that will help her grow. Being positive about yourself will influence your daughter's internal dialogue and help her develop positive thoughts about herself. So improving your own sense of self-worth can affect your daughter in a positive way. Any work you do to improve yourself is a gift you give to yourself and your children.

#5 Have High but Reasonable Expectations

Having high expectations will help your daughter realize the importance of aiming high. It will encourage her to try to achieve her goals and dreams. The high expectations parents have for their daughters should be set with the assumption that she will make her best effort at everything she attempts and should be consistent with the goals your daughter sets for herself.

Parents who have high expectations and spend time with their offspring have children who achieve at higher levels than other children.

National Institute of Child Health and Development, "How Do Children Spend Their Time? Children's Activities, School Achievements, and Well-Being" *Today's Issue*, August 2000, page 1–2.

Girls who are under too much pressure burn out or lose interest in a previously enjoyable activity because their parents have unreasonable expectations. When parents push their daughters to be perfect and compare their daughters to others they erode their daughter's self-esteem. Girls have said to me, "I am trying so hard to please my parents, but it is never enough." Other girls have confided to me that their parents' expectations are not in line with their own expectations for themselves. "She wants me to be a teacher and I just don't want to be a teacher. I try to talk to her but every time I mention another profession she finds everything negative about it," said one seventeen-year-old.

Staying connected with your daughter through effective communication will help parents maintain a high standard that is consistent with their daughter's aspirations. If your daughter has not set any goals, then sitting down with her and helping her come up with specific, measurable goals would help her greatly.

A CONSIDERATION FOR PARENTS

As we all know, parenting is a continuous balancing act. It takes effort to maintain an atmosphere where your daughter is able to develop optimal self-esteem. This is not an environment where they think they are important because of material things such as money or clothes; instead it is an environment where they feel they are important because they are loved, heard, and honored as human beings.

#6 Encourage Problem Solving

As frustrating or uncomfortable as it may be for you, your daughter will inevitably experience difficulties in her life that are painful for her. One common situation is conflict with her peers. One week she is accepted in a group, and the next week she is not. One week Susie is her best friend, then the next week she can't stand to be with Susie.

It is important to control your unconscious reactions or your desire to retaliate against the nine-year-old who keeps harassing your daughter. Remain objective. Keep your composure and keep the situation in perspective. Remind yourself to listen first (seek first to understand) and to offer advice only when asked.

Guide your daughter through these conflicts. Avoid encouraging her to find blame or play the victim role. Instead, help her understand her contribution to the situation and analyze what she can do differently. In other words, encourage her to come up with appropriate solutions by utilizing effective communication.

Although conflicts with friends are difficult, these situations create teaching opportunities. Under your guidance, your daughter can learn to establish healthy boundaries for herself, for example. You can help her to believe that she has control of difficult situations in her life and that her worth cannot be determined by someone else's actions or words.

Role-play and discuss how she will act in certain circumstances with her friends. These scenarios might include what she will be do in a situation involving drinking or drugs or even sex. Deciding and rehearsing with you what she will say in these instances will give her confidence when she actually has to face these issues. And she will have to face them.

A few high-school girls once confided in me that they were afraid of what would happen at college drinking parties. So I sat down with these girls and we brainstormed ideas about how they could handle these parties. They role-played with each other. When they went off to college, they reported back to me that they felt more "in control" of their behavior when they were at these parties. "Knowing what I was going to do in the situation was a huge relief to me," said one teen.

#7 Encourage Your Daughter to Recognize Her Feelings

When your daughter is upset or excited, encourage her to acknowledge the existence of those feelings and allow herself to feel them. Telling her to settle down or minimizing her emotions confuses your daughter. She doesn't know how to feel.

If she is having negative emotions, encourage your daughter to face the feelings and see if they are resulting in the behavior or result that she wants. If not, encourage her to express it, accept it, and let it go. Repressed negative emotions are linked to diseases such as heart disease, stroke, depression, and so on. Explain to your daughter that negative feelings such as anger, sadness, fear, and guilt are normal and that she can use them as a signal that something needs to be changed.

#8 Maintain Appropriate Physical Contact

Moms and dads should continue to hug and kiss their daughters during adolescence as a way to show that they love them. Affection from both parents benefits girls, but I feel that the dad's role warrants additional discussion here.

At a presentation given by Steve Biddulph, author of *Raising Boys,* he commented on the fact that a father plays a major role in the development of his daughter's self-esteem. A dad's role deserves much consideration during adolescence, when the relationship between mom and daughter is likely to become strained.

When a healthy relationship and connection exists between a dad and his daughter, the girl is likely grow up knowing that she is capable of being loved and respected by someone of the opposite sex. Joe Kelly, who has twin daughters, says, "Any girl is going to actually want to know what is interesting to and what gets the attention of the opposite sex. How I react to her, how I act around her is going to be really crucial."

Unfortunately, many dads shy away from their daughter when she begins puberty and starts to develop physically. When a dad sees his daughter turning into a young woman, he may feel self-conscious and uncomfortable and not know what to do. Many times they take a step back from their relationship.

Dads may feel discomfort with the fact that their daughter is developing into a woman. One dad summed it up when he said, "I felt odd looking at my daughter and thinking that she looks good. Not in a sexual way, but noticing her physical development made me feel uncomfortable." Another dad added, "I just kept thinking, I remember what I was thinking when I looked at girls her age who were attractive, and it scared me to think guys would be look-ing at my daughter like that. I felt myself pulling away because I didn't want to face these thoughts."

Whatever the reasons behind these feelings, dads can get past their insecurity or discomfort. When they do, they tend to stay in touch emotionally and physically with their daughter. When a father pulls away, the daughter wonders what she did to make her dad not want to be with her as much as he had in

A study of thirty-six hundred children revealed that one factor linked to school achievement and emotional adjustment was the development of "warm relationships" between parent and child. Characteristics of a warm relationship included the parents hugging their children often and telling them that they loved them and were proud of them. These children were less withdrawn, had fewer behavioral problems, and were happier than other children in the study.

(*Healthy Environments, Healthy Families* by Sandra Hofferth at University of Michigan, Institute for Social Research)

the past. A dad's retreat from his daughter's life may cause her to have difficulty with relationships with men later in life. Her self-esteem may suffer as a result because she does not feel capable of being loved. Consider the following letter written by a teen.

Dad,

I am writing this letter because I have noticed that you are not around as much as you used to be. You and I used to laugh all the time. You would totally crack me up.

Lately, it's like you don't want to be around me anymore. If I did something to make you mad, I'm sorry. I miss your hugs. I miss just going for a walk by ourselves.

I miss talking to you and listening to your stupid jokes.

I hope I didn't do anything to make you mad. I know I do a lot of stuff with my friends. I hope that doesn't make you mad.

Can we be friends again, Dad?

By staying in touch physically, a dad can give his daughter a feeling of comfort when she faces the unrealistic ideal of female beauty in our society. Appropriate physical contact can include a hug, a gentle touch on the arm or shoulder, a kiss on the cheek, or a clasp of her hand. When you show her affection, you help your daughter form a healthy image of herself and boost her ability to feel loved.

Work (with the help of a therapist, if necessary) to get past your uncomfortable feelings about your daughter's budding sexuality, for her sake. If she doesn't find affection at home, she may go out and try to fill the void by being promiscuous.

#9 Encourage and Discuss Your Daughter's Goals and Dreams

Take time to talk with your daughter about what she wants to be or what she wants to study in school. Ask her questions such as "What do you think your purpose in life is?" "Do you see yourself being married and having kids?" "Will you have a career?" "Do you see yourself doing both?" "What kinds of things do you want to accomplish in your life?"

The most important part of this interaction for you is listening. Allow your daughter to dream big.

#10 Look into Her Eyes

At least once or twice a day look into your daughter's eyes in a way that communicates that you love her. Doing so will encourage an unspoken connectedness between you and help her feel loved. Hold the gaze for just a few seconds; you don't have to say a word. Parents who have tried this technique say that their daughter suddenly opens up and starts talking, or that they both end up giggling instead of fighting.

When she has difficulty meeting your eye contact, she may be struggling with some problem—something that you may be able to address with her using your effective communication skills.

#11 Make Positive Comments to Others

When your daughter is within earshot, say something positive about her character to someone else, "I am proud of my daughter's performance, and what I love most about her is how thoughtful she can be with others," for example. Your making these kinds of comments to others shows her that you mean what you are saying, because you didn't have to say anything at all.

#12 Make Positive Comments to Her Just Because

When she's not expecting it, tell your daughter, "Hey, I just wanted to remind you that I love you," give her a kiss on the cheek, and walk away. She might think, "Oh my gosh, what's happening to Mom/Dad?" but it's always good to keep them guessing! Every now and then, let her know that you think about her often during the day. Send emails or leave little notes on the bathroom mirror or on her bed.

#13 Model a Balanced Life and Discuss Its Importance

Share with your daughter that you are striving to find a healthy balance in your life and discuss the importance of this process.

Let her know that maintaining balance in your life helps alleviate stress and allows you to get done what is necessary as well as spend time with family and friends. Ask her if she thinks her life is balanced or how she thinks you are doing at living a balanced life.

#14 Discuss the Difference between Self-Esteem, Self-Confidence, Self-Image, and Conceit

Share with her information about the development of self-esteem and how it differs from self-confidence, self-image, and conceit. Ask her what self-esteem issues or development she notices in her friends or in herself. Share with her that you are trying to help her develop a healthy internal feedback mechanism so that she gradually turns to herself for approval rather than to others.

#15 Schedule a Girls' Night Out or a Dad-And-Daughter Night Out

On a regular basis, schedule a special night out for your daughter with just mom or just dad. This one-on-one time is perfect for asking questions and discussing different topics. It is also a perfect opportunity for you to practice listening skills.

Spending time with just one parent and no siblings may be a treat for your daughter as well.

#16 Each Night Spend Fifteen to Thirty Minutes with Each Child

If possible, do some of the activities below:

- ❀ Sit at the edge of her bed and chat.
- ❀ Read or tell her a story.
- ❀ Give her a massage on her back or shoulders.
- ❀ Ask her opinion about something.

#17 Find an Opportunity for Her to Teach You Something

Give your daughter a chance to teach you something she has learned, whether it's how to do a layup shot in basketball, how to use the computer, or what the heck a theorem in geometry is. This will boost her confidence and encourage her to feel that what she learns is important.

#18 Foster Her Internal Feedback System

Ask your daughter how she felt about something someone said to her, good or bad. Encourage her to look inside herself for answers and let her know that she can find a solution to every problem. Help her to realize that she can make a difference in her life and the lives of others.

#19 Support Her Opinions and Decisions When Possible

Although you may not agree with everything she says or believes, encourage her to come up with her own opinions.

Look for opportunities to support her decisions. When you do not agree with her and have to put your foot down, give her an explanation. She probably won't like it, but at least you are promoting communication.

As she reaches her later teenage years and into her early twenties, your daughter may make decisions that you do not support. Keep the lines of communication open and let her know what you're thinking.

#20 Encourage Extracurricular Activities

Many studies in recent years have linked high self-esteem to extracurricular activities such as sports, music, and membership in associations such as the Girl Scouts of America. Your daughter's involvement in these activities may improve her self-confidence, and participation in sports might help her body image as well.

Extracurricular activities allow your daughter to learn valuable life skills, such as persistence, working with others, setting goals, and self-discipline, all of which can positively affect your daughter's self-esteem. When done in moderation, extracurricular activities can be a positive addition to your daughter's life.

Be careful, though: defining your child by the roles she plays can lead her to believe that her performance in these roles determines her self-worth. In addition to complimenting her on her performance, tell your daughter that you are lucky to have her in your life because she is a kind, lovable, and capable person.

The development of optimal self-esteem is an ongoing process for your daughter. Staying connected and nurturing your daughter's development of self-esteem is important even during the rough times.

○ ○ ○

Conflicts

My mother is a psychiatric nurse by training. I usually tell people that she must have gone into this field in an attempt to figure out her kids! I remember her telling me that she and I would start to experience some conflicts when I became a teenager. I recall thinking, "No way. That will never happen." You see, my mom was my coach and my role model (and she still is today). I looked up to her and loved her. How could things change?

Fast forward a few years, to an evening when I came home from high school. I was sixteen years old. My mom was doing the dishes (probably because one of us conveniently forgot to do them after dinner) and we began to argue. What started the argument I don't recall. The argument escalated and I said some very harsh things. I know I didn't use profanity because we were never allowed to, but I am sure I wasn't lacking in sarcasm. All of a sudden, I looked across the room and stopped my tirade just as quickly as I had started. Although my mom's back was to me, I could see by the slight quiver in her body that she was crying. The only other time I had witnessed my mom crying was at her mother's funeral when I was six years old.

I remember feeling a tremendous amount of guilt standing in the kitchen and could not move from the spot where I was standing. After what seemed like an hour, I gradually moved from my spot and dragged myself up the stairs. I sank into my bed and sobbed into my pillow thinking, "How could I say those things to her?" I hadn't intended to hurt her, but I know that I did, very badly.

My mom and I did not talk about that day until I began to conduct research for this book. I thought, who better to interview about raising girls than my own mom? During our interview, we sat for a while and chatted, and then I got up the nerve to ask her if she remembered the episode in the kitchen. Before I even finished my question she replied, "Yes, I do remember." I asked with hesitation, "Do you remember what we fought about?" And she replied, "No, but I do remember what you said to me." Not sure I wanted to hear the answer to this next question, I said, "Oh, really. What did I say?" She replied, "I remember that you said you hated me."

I was shocked. I do not recall telling my mom that I hated her. But that was her perception of what happened that night in the kitchen. In fact, that was how she perceived my actions throughout most of my teenage years. Yet, even though I acted that way toward her, she still loved me unconditionally.

Where Does This Behavior Come From?

Why did I act that way toward my mother? Why does your daughter verbally attack you or roll her eyes when you give her your opinion? Or is your relationship nonexistent?

This chapter discusses the common sources of conflict, some inevitable and some unnecessary, between parents and their daughter. As you will see, even though the problems seem to spring up overnight, this is simply not the case. Many kinds of situations and contributing factors can slowly build up, resulting in conflict.

The goal of this chapter is not to cast blame on anyone, but instead to allow you to take a closer look at the role you are playing in your daughter's life and learn how you may be contributing to unnecessary conflict. This chapter will also cover the types of conflicts you can expect to deal with during your daughter's adolescence. Take this opportunity to travel back in time to your adolescent years. Attempt to recognize feelings you experienced, and remember how your parents acted toward you. Then you'll be less likely to repeat your parents' negative actions, focusing instead on treating your daughter in a positive way.

Being aware of inevitable conflicts will prepare you and allow you to protect yourself and your daughter from unnecessary suffering. Taking a good look at yourself and the role you play in your daughter's life and its dramas may enable you to avoid needless conflict that zaps your energy.

What Is Your Role?

In the first decade of life you were your daughter's protector. You could do no wrong. She trusted you to be her source of truth. Now, as your daughter begins to climb the proverbial mountain toward adulthood, she needs you to instruct her less and protect her less from all bad things. She needs you to support her in both good times and bad. Act as her safety net and her guide through the tumultuous journey ahead. Help her develop the skills to make responsible decisions about relationships, drugs, and other complex issues. Girls need their parents to try to understand their position, their thoughts, and their feelings rather than telling them what their position, thoughts, and feelings should be.

Consider making a conscious decision to change your parental role as your daughter enters adolescence. If you continue in the same role you have always played you will undoubtedly experience more conflict with your daughter than necessary. Mother Nature is changing your daughter. She has no choice in the matter. You, the parent, do have a choice. You can make the choice to change right along with her.

Conflict and change are facts of life during adolescence. Your daughter is in conflict with you and with herself. Her body and her mind are constantly changing and many girls complain that it is hard for them to keep up with all of the changes. Conflict and change are necessary for your daughter's development, both physical and emotional. Your daughter must test the boundaries, exercise her independence, and try to determine how she will fit into society. Each parent and child will experience this conflict in varying degrees. If a parent wants to decrease or prevent needless conflict, it may be time to analyze what his or her role in the conflict has been, what it presently is, and what the parent wants his or her role to be.

Inevitable Conflicts

The conflicts that are discussed below are inevitable. As you read them, ask yourself how you have handled these conflicts in the past or how you will handle them in the future.[1]

Liberation toward Independence

As your daughter journeys through adolescence she will attempt to liberate herself from you in order to establish her independence. However, this does not mean she no longer needs you. In fact, although she is less likely to tell you, she needs you now more than ever. She needs you to assume a different role than the role you have played for the first decade or so of her life. This new role involves transitioning from being the controlling figure in her life to becoming a guide. While maintaining effective communication and staying connected, you will watch her grow into a young woman from the sidelines.

During this liberation period you can expect her to disagree with almost everything you say. One frustrated parent wrote, "When I say the tablecloth is white, she will say it is off-white. If I say the chair is black, she will say it is charcoal."

As the daughter liberates herself from her parents, she takes a very critical look at her mom's life and, as a result, her mom may receive the brunt of the attack. She wants to be independent of her mother and to seek a different path. One girl commented, "Sometimes with my mom, I get so angry because I see so much more for myself then being a wife and mother. But then when I think about it, I wouldn't want my mom to be any different than what she is." Another girl said, "I always get so angry at my mom. I say things I don't mean. I don't know why I do it." Your once-sweet little girl wants to show you that she is not like you. At times she challenges everything about you. One mom exclaimed, "When my daughter started going through adolescence she would look at me as if I had two heads!"

When her world starts to expand and she comes in contact with new influences, such as friends, teachers, and society at large, your daughter will begin to notice your shortcomings and every mistake that you make. You are not perfect and she may be angry with you because of that. As she liberates herself from you, your flaws make it easier for her to do so. One mother summed it up when she said, "I think Mother Nature prepares teenagers for leaving home by allowing them to see that their parents are less than perfect."

Knowing this, expect your daughter to challenge everything about you: your clothes, your hair, your ideas, and your life, anything that will show that she is not like you. It is much easier to respond to this type of confrontation when you actually like your clothes, your hair, your ideas, and your life. Excessive pain felt as a result of your daughter's comments may suggest some unresolved issues in yourself that you should investigate.

This liberation of the child is anything but freeing for the parent. It may be frustrating or challenging when this happens, but knowing that it is likely to happen can help a parent prepare to not take it personally.

Use of "I" Statements

Be prepared for this trying time in your lives and instead of allowing it to upset you, bring your daughter's unkind statements to her attention by using "I" statements. For example, you could say something like, "Honey, I know you are going through a time when you want to be completely opposite from me. That is normal and I understand it. I went through the same thing with my mom. But when you constantly disagree with me I feel _____." (You fill in the blank.)

Your daughter may still look at you as though you have two heads, but you have planted the seed of empathy. If her unpleasant behavior continues and you just cannot take it anymore, you may also want to say, "How do you think you would feel if I constantly disagreed with you and told you that you were wrong?" If she answers, "You *do* always disagree with me and tell me that I am wrong," then you may have some evaluating of your own to do. Otherwise, she may not answer your question, but she may begin to think about it and eventually change her behavior.

In the meantime, avoid getting upset about every comment she makes and don't attempt to make her empathize with you every minute of the day. Accepting that your adolescent daughter will think you are out of touch most of the time may decrease unnecessary hurt and anger for you. "When I stopped fighting with my daughter and started replying to her comments with things like, 'Well, that's your opinion, darling' it seemed to decrease my anger and my daughter's need to contin-ually challenge me," stated a mother of a fifteen-year-old girl.

The Need for Privacy

Remember your adolescence and recall the excitement, horror, and uncertainty you felt as your body changed. You began to lock the bathroom door and didn't want anyone to see you naked. Your thoughts and feelings about your world were no longer conveyed to your parents but to your friends. Your voice would quiet down to a hush whenever your mom, dad, or siblings came around while you were talking to a friend on the phone. Everything became a big secret from your family.

A parent who has had an exceptionally close relationship with her daughter up until adolescence can be very hurt by this sudden need for privacy. She may even try to make her daughter feel guilty about not including her anymore.

Wanting privacy is a normal part of adolescence. Your daughter needs her privacy as she develops physically and emotionally. If you are taking this personally then you may want to consider why. Maybe you are hurt by the loss of a confidante or you feel that you are no longer as important in your daughter's life. It is common to feel this way, but as one girl put it, "I wish my mom would just get over it! She wants to be my best friend and when I talk to my friends instead of her she gets all messed up."

With effective communication your relationship can still flourish. You are no longer the center of your daughter's world, and she needs you to remain present on the sidelines during this time. Continue to support her, and allow her some room to grow and experience new relationships and activities. As one mother of three daughters said, "I learned that I had to let my daughters go and be there for them in a different way than I had in the past. What I also learned is that when you make an effort to maintain a connection they eventually come back to you."

Selfish and Self-Centered

As your daughter approaches adolescence you will undoubtedly see signs of self-centeredness. It has always amazed me how an adolescent girl can be completely oblivious to any part of a person's life that is unrelated to her. While coaching I would often have to remind girls, "I do have a life away from you," or "It would be nice if you would consider how that affects me." These girls would typically respond, "Oh, yeah. I forgot," or "What?" accompanied by a look of bewilderment. Many times this self-centered attitude angered me, but when I began to think about it, I realized that they probably really did forget. Everyone experiences phases in life where they must be self-centered because they are trying to determine their identity and what role they play in this life. As they mature and grow more comfortable with their place in the world and their importance, they become better able to consider other people's lives outside of their own and how their actions affect others.

As parents, however, we should remind our adolescent daughters to consider the feelings and needs of others. I have found that when I consistently send this message, it begins to sink in over time. Firm but gentle reminders such as "Yes, dear, I know you perceive this to be best for you, but what about your siblings? Your teacher? Your mom and dad?" can be effective. Let your daughter know that considering the feelings of others will enable her to be an effective communicator. Also discuss the fact that you, as a parent, make decisions every day in which you try to consider her feelings and needs.

Don't expect your adolescent to be happy about the fact that she must consider others in her decision making. To think about the needs of others goes against her nature at this point in her life.

Self-centered behavior may signal to the parent that the daughter needs to exercise more control over her life. Encourage opportunities for individual decision making in order to give your daughter a sense of control. If she is constantly having to conform to other people's wishes, considerations, or rules during a time when she needs to gain control over herself and her life, she may resort to unhealthy ways of getting control, such as aggressive behavior, eating disorders, self-mutilation, unhealthy relationships, and so on. The trick is to give her healthy opportunities to control her own life so that she does not seek unhealthy or unacceptable forms of control.

Girls reveal that the more their parents accuse them of being self-centered or selfish the more self-centered and selfish they choose to be. She may sometimes act this way as an instinctual reaction to your comments. Other times she may do it consciously to irritate you because she knows it bothers you. Or as one seventeen-year-old said to me, "I am such a brat to my parents sometimes because they never let me make any decisions. Everything has to be their way. I am almost an adult. Can't they let me make some of my own decisions?"

Allowing your daughter to make decisions about her room, her subjects in school, her future career aspirations, or her extracurricular activities will enable her to feel that she has control of her home environment and her future. Give her choices when setting appropriate ground rules like curfews and chores around the house. One mom stated, "When my daughter was in her early teens and she wanted to go to a party that I did not feel was appropriate for her to attend, I gave her options like having friends over to our house for a small get-together or going out to a movie with her friends and ice cream after at our house."

Remember that her self-centeredness is an inevitable stage. She must go through it in order to establish her independence. Remind yourself that you are in this for the long run and that changes do not happen overnight. Consistent messages over a period of time will eventually sink in.

Conflicts with Friends

As your daughter's social focus moves from family to friends, she may experience challenges in her relationships. Conflicts among girls are common and can affect your daughter's self-esteem. Many girls link how they feel about themselves with what their friends think of them. Guiding your daughter through the rough spots while giving her enough latitude to choose her own friends can strengthen your relationship.

Don't Approve of Her Friends?

What do you do if you do not like your daughter's friends? The first step is to accept that your daughter, not you, needs to decide whom she will spend time with. You cannot control her every move or decision. Talk with her about your concerns. Expect resistance and tell her that you understand her defensive reaction. Say that you are an observer looking in and this is what you see. Let her know that it is ultimately her decision who her friends are and that these people have an impact on how she feels about herself. Encourage her to surround herself with friends who support her goals and dreams in life. Then be aware of opportunities to subtly discuss these friends with her. For example, if she says, "Laura told so-and-so that she is just a nerd," refrain from saying, "I never liked that Laura. You really shouldn't hang around with her, you know." Instead, try asking her, "How do you think so-and-so felt when Laura called her that?" or "How would you feel if Laura said that about you?" or "If Laura says things like that about other people, how do you know she is not saying that about you when you are not around?" Let her come to her own conclusions about Laura but lay the groundwork first.

A fourteen-year-old girl wrote to me, "My mom told me she really didn't want me to spend time with my friend Jessica. She said she was worried that I would get into the same trouble that Jess got into. She told me it was my decision because she knew she couldn't control who my friends were. For some stupid reason, I started to see Jess differently. Eventually I lost touch with her. I guess my mom was right."

Another girl emailed, "My dad told me I was forbidden to play with my friend Monica because he didn't like her. He didn't even know her. He only knows what my mom told him. So instead of listening to him I still played with Monica just to show him!"

You will not be able to choose every person your daughter comes in contact with. This being said, you can still monitor her decisions by communicating with her effectively. But the less pressure you put on her to do something a certain way, the more likely she will be to do it your way. If you force your opinions on her by using the old "I am the parent and as long as you live in my house you will live by my rules" approach, you will push her away and she will do what you do not want her to do, either out of spite or as a result of feeling unsupported. Without a doubt, occasionally you must put your foot down. But if all you are doing is putting your foot down, you may end up with a daughter who resents you, and a very sore foot!

If You Can't Beat 'Em, Invite Them Over

Getting to know your daughter's friend by inviting her to stay at your house for the night or day may help you get to know another side of your daughter's friend and change your mind about her. Or it may reinforce your gut feeling about her, good or bad. Either way, this will give you an opportunity to see how this person treats your daughter and vice versa. Spending time around this person will help you gather information that you can bring up at another time when you are discussing your daughter's friends.

Avoid putting down your daughter's friends even if you do not like them. Constantly reminding your daughter that you do not like her friends will discourage communication between you and ultimately push her closer to the friends you don't like.

And finally, if you consistently surround yourself with people who support you and treat you with respect, you will model for your daughter how to choose appropriate friends.

Mother-Daughter Conflict

Many of the conflicts throughout adolescence seem to occur between mother and daughter. To be sure, dads and daughters have their difficulties as well, but moms and daughters tend to have a more volatile relationship throughout adolescence.[2]

Why does this happen? A mother and daughter may look, sound, and act like each other. This similarity is the biggest obstacle a daughter can see between her and her independence. People are beginning to tell her how much she looks like her mother and this drives her crazy.

When I ask girls why they become irritated with these comments, they say, "I want people to tell me I am my own person. I am tired of hearing I am just like . . . her!" Looking back at my own adolescence I can see that I wanted to be liberated from the constraints I felt the mother-daughter relationship had placed on me. I realize now that these constraints were necessary to teach me and to protect me. But the adolescent wants less constraint, more freedom, and more individuality and her mom tends to represent the unresolved issues the daughter is dealing with herself.

The young girl is trying to determine the person she will become and recently she has realized that her mom is human and doesn't know everything. This adds fuel to the fire, especially if the life that her mom has chosen is not to the liking of her daughter.

As an adult, Jan had many altercations with her mom but had never understood why. Finally, after much deliberation and a few counseling sessions, Jan was able to come to grips with her unconscious anger toward her mom. When Jan was growing up, her father worked, came home, read the paper, and watched television. Rarely would he help her mom with household duties even though Jan's mom had a full-time job herself. Jan's dad would bellow orders to her mom and the kids from his chair in the living room and her mom would scurry about to meet his needs.

Jan finally figured out that she was angry at her mom for allowing herself to be treated that way by her father. Jan recalls telling her mom that she would never allow her husband to behave that way toward her. The interesting fact is Jan failed to express much, if any, anger toward her father. In fact, Jan's anger toward her father for treating her mom disrespectfully was misplaced onto her mom. Jan also envisioned more opportunities for herself and for her mom and was frustrated that her mom didn't change her situation. Jan may also have been reacting out of fear that if she became a mother and wife she would have to become like her mother.

Mothers often receive the greater part of their daughter's anger because they are the easiest target. Expect this behavior and understand that the anger may be masking fear and frustration. Armed with this information, a mom can help her daughter work through some of these feelings and develop healthy coping mechanisms. Looking past the behavior to the real issue will save mom and daughter some hurt feelings and unnecessary arguments and bring the two closer together.

Dad's Role in Mother-Daughter Conflicts

The father's role in raising a daughter is often undervalued.[3] A wonderful relationship can flourish if a dad stays connected with his daughter. Joe Kelly, executive director of Dads and Daughters, explains, "Fathers play a very unique and key role"[4] in girls' lives.

But many dads simply don't know what to do when conflicts between mother and daughter arise. Out of fear, frustration, or a need to fix the problem, he may unintentionally make things worse by doing one or all of the following:

- ❀ Dad retreats into his own world and offers no support to either mother or daughter. He does not understand what is going on and, thinking it must be "secret women's business," he avoids becoming a part of it.

- ❀ Dad sides with his wife in the conflict, possibly destroying communication with his daughter in the future.

- ❀ Dad sides with his daughter and undermines the mom's authority, resulting in some serious negative consequences in the marriage relationship. In addition, the daughter may feel that she has power over her mother because she has her dad on her side.

While gathering information for this book, I interviewed fathers who had healthy relationships with both their wives and their adult daughters. These men gave valuable advice about what to do when their wife and daughter experienced conflicts, which I have summarized below.

If at all possible stay out of the argument when it is happening. Only intervene if disrespect is being shown by the daughter. If the father intervenes by saying, "Please do not talk to your mother that way," followed by, "This problem is between the two of you and you need to work it out yourselves," he will be able to stay on the sidelines and not get involved just yet. Do not intervene at this time if the mother is being disrespectful. Discuss that privately with her later.

One father told me he doesn't like to jump into the argument and attack his daughter because "the daughter isn't always the one who is 100 percent in the wrong." (This philosophy applies to disagreements between father and daughter as well.) The parent on the outside of the argument does not necessarily know the full story. Underlying issues that he is not aware of may be at work. It is usually best to allow the people involved to work it out without interference, unless the daughter is acting disrespectful.

After the altercation is finished, the father can make himself an ally to both his daughter and his wife when he approaches his daughter after the disagreement. He can ask her how she could have handled the situation differently and talk to her about what helps him communicate with her mom, thus encouraging his daughter to work it out with her mom. He should not undermine his wife's position or any decision she has made regarding her daughter. The advice he gives his daughter should be about how to work things out with her mom. Here is how a conversation between father and daughter might go:

Daughter	*Mom isn't fair. She doesn't listen.*
Dad	*Obviously you're upset and after you calm down you and your mom can work this out.*
Daughter	*I don't want to work it out. She's impossible. She expects too much.*

Dad	*It sounds as though you're feeling overwhelmed. This is something you need to share with your mother. Remember, we both have high expectations of you. Your mother loves you and wants the best for you. She knows you're capable and she believes in you. If you are feeling overwhelmed, talk to her about that and you can work toward a solution together.*

Dads can also help prevent altercations by listening to their daughter's concerns and encouraging them to communicate with mom before the blowup happens.

Daughter	*Dad, can I talk to you?*
Dad	*Sure, what's up?*
Daughter	*Well, Mom is driving me crazy. She sets these strict time limits for my homework and bedtime and I can't handle it. Can you talk to her for me?*
Dad	*It sounds like you're frustrated. What do you think Mom should do instead?*
Daughter	*I think she should let me make some of my own decisions.*
Dad	*That seems reasonable. Does your mom know how you feel?*
Daughter	*I don't know. I haven't said anything to her yet. I don't want her to get mad.*
Dad	*So you're worried about making her angry, but if you don't talk to her you'll continue to be angry. Is that right?*
Daughter	*Well, I was hoping you would talk to her for me.*
Dad	*I could do that, but my talking to her won't really help either of you. You two need to work this out with each other. If you'd like I can pretend to be Mom and you can practice saying to me what you're going to say to her. How does that sound?*
Daughter	*Okay, I'll give it a try.*

◉

Husband and Father

The father can also support his wife. He can tell her that she is a good mother and that he believes she and her daughter can work this out. It's probably best not to offer unsolicited advice on how to handle the daughter or tell his wife what she does wrong when she is upset. Let her calm down, then ask her later how she thought the situation went. If your wife is upset about what happened, ask her how she could have handled it differently. Suggest that she sit down with your daughter to discuss what happened and search for a solution when they have both calmed down.

As a husband, the dad's role is to support his wife's decisions and to encourage the mother and daughter to work out their issues together.

As a father, the dad's role is to listen, give advice when asked, and reassure his daughter. He should support his wife's decisions while helping his daughter understand the importance of working out the problem with her mother. As I stated previously, dads should avoid taking sides. Nevertheless, if the mother has made a decision regarding a consequence for the daughter, the dad should go along with this mandate. If he disagrees with the mother, that discussion is best conducted between the parents in private. If changing a consequence proves necessary because the consequence is not consistent with family values or made out of anger or spite then whoever set the

Dads may reply to the above advice and say, "I can't do that. My wife and I have decided that we will present a united front." If by united front they mean that each parent supports the other's decisions, I condone it wholeheartedly. But if they mean that when the mother and daughter have a conflict they take the mom's side or refuse to discuss the situation with the daughter, then the "united front" will discourage communication between parents and their daughters.

consequence should be the one to talk to the daughter about the change.

Tips to Help Yourself Cope with the Inevitable

The following tips, recommended by parents of older girls, will help you prepare yourself for and cope with the inevitable conflicts during adolescence.

Take Care of Yourself

During the times when you feel things are just not going well, give yourself a break. Remind yourself that you are doing the best you can. Use this opportunity to get in touch with yourself. Explore your own self-esteem, self-image, and body image. Work on areas that need to be addressed, and strive for balance in your life.

Go out for coffee with friends. Get a massage. Read a book. Take a few minutes behind closed doors to recharge. Do something that you enjoy. Try to do something, big or small, for yourself every day. By taking care of yourself you will set a great example for your daughter; she will recognize the importance of listening to and developing her own spirit. In addition, you will have more energy and strength to handle stressful situations in all parts of your life.

Talk to Other Parents

Talking to other parents helps you see that you are not alone in dealing with thorny issues concerning your adolescent girl. Each family has their own problems to deal with. When you talk to other parents, you might even find that your situation is not all that bad.

A word of caution though: Often I hear parents complaining about their daughters to each other, many times while their daughters are present. The girls respond by muttering, "Do they think I can't hear them?" or "Hello, I am standing right here." Emphasizing daughters' negative qualities to other adults damages your daughter's self-esteem and reinforces to the adolescent that adults as a whole do not understand them.

Avoid Taking It Personally

When your daughter opens an old emotional wound or touches on an insecurity you possess, you might take this personally and feel hurt or angry. Instead of taking it out on yourself, your daughter, or your family, try to recognize the underlying issue causing you to have these feelings. Work through your own issues by seeing a counselor, attending seminars, reading self-help books, writing in a journal, or talking to a trusted friend or your spouse. You will thereby lessen the unnecessary pain you experience throughout your entire life, not just during your daughter's adolescence.

If your daughter says she hates you or makes other hurtful statements, sit down with her and share your feelings about these comments. If your daughter says, "You are so weird," just smile, remember that this is a part of adolescence, and quietly pray that she will have her own adolescent girl one day!

Utilize Mentors

Your daughter needs to have appropriate adult female role models and mentors as she goes through adolescence. Encourage these relationships and make an effort to meet the person she has chosen as her mentor. Listen to what your daughter says about her. Invite her over to your house for dinner so you can get to know her.

If feelings of jealousy creep in and cause you to want to sever the relationship, ask yourself why you may be reacting this way. Acting jealous and speaking negatively about her mentor will only push your daughter closer to that person and build resentment toward you. Stay connected with your daughter and monitor the relationship from a distance.

A sixteen-year-old girl said, "Before I go out and try something I am not too sure of, I like to ask my friend's mom what she thinks about it. I don't ask my parents because I don't want them to take the car away or think I can't handle it. My parents don't have a clue about what I deal with every day. It is just easier to ask my friend's mom because she listens to me." A fifteen-year-old commented, "sometimes I talk to other adults because I want to hear other opinions. I hear my parents telling me the same thing over and over again and I just want to run it by someone who doesn't know my whole life history."

Divorce

Sometimes a divorcing parent may not think he or she has the strength to attend to the child's needs. If this is true for you, it may be a good idea to consider seeking the help of a professional who can assess the child's needs, as well as a family member or mentor who can help her through the grieving process.

Parents need to consider putting their feelings aside at times and communicate with the child so she does not feel she is losing both parents. When one parent moves out or loses contact with the child, the parent remaining can connect with the child to help her feel secure in their particular relationship. If a parent has feelings of resentment toward the parent who has left, he or she must not impose those feelings on the child. A parent involved in a divorce situation should not try to sabotage the relationship between the other parent and the child. The divorce is between the adults, not the child and adult.

DIVORCE: A GRIEVING PROCESS FOR ADULT AND CHILD

When divorce happens, every member of the family experiences grief. Just as the mother and father are grieving the loss of the relationship, so is the child. Although the process of grief may involve the same stages for each individual, each person does not experience the same feelings at the same time or in the same way. After all, the relationship between parent and child differs greatly from the relationship between spouses. The timing and reasons for grief will vary for parent and child. The parent has to try to understand each child and allow each child his or her own space to grieve at his or her own pace.

Unnecessary Conflicts

Some conflicts, although common, can be avoided if you do a bit of soul-searching and become conscious of your actions. Identifying the unnecessary conflict and recognizing your part in it is the first step toward eliminating the conflict. Committing to work on underlying issues and dealing with destructive feelings comprises the second step.

In order to take the first step, let's explore ways to try to identify your experiences from your own adolescence that may be contributing to unnecessary conflict between you and your daughter.

Get in Touch with Your Past

In order to see things from your daughter's perspective, consider revisiting the feelings and situations that you dealt with during your adolescence.[5] While this may not give you a complete picture of what your daughter has to endure, it will allow you to begin to empathize with her instead of being constantly angry or irritated at her.

If your relationship with your mom or dad was difficult, avoid dwelling on it. That is not the purpose of this exercise. Although these feelings may surface during your exploration, try to put them on hold for now until you can deal with them directly. For now, simply try to recall how you felt during adolescence.

You may recall yourself swearing that you would never treat your child the way your parents treated you. As an adult now, looking back, you can analyze these adolescent thoughts and decide whether they are valid now that you are an adult as well as a parent. Admit that you and your parents had some difficult times if this is true, and then remember you have the power to change your behavior with your own children. Acknowledge your problematic behavior and the changes you can make to improve your relationship with your daughter. Recognizing unhealthy or unproductive patterns within yourself and changing them will allow you to eliminate unnecessary pain for you and your daughter.

You may find yourself struggling to recall some of your feelings and experiences from your adolescence. Read on for some suggested ways to spark your memory.

Methods to Get in Touch with Your Past

Dig up some old pictures of yourself, your friends, and your family from that period of your life. Pull out old notes or letters from your high-school friends (come on, I know you have them somewhere) as well as yearbooks, awards, and keepsakes from that era. Ask your parents if they have kept any of your old notebooks or report cards. If you want to be really creative, make a collage using the memorabilia you find.

Call up an old friend you haven't talked to in years. (If you don't have the person's current telephone number, try contacting your high school's alumni association to see if they have current contact information for that person. You can also try the Internet.) Talk to your friend(s) about the old days and ask whether he or she remembers anything in particular you said or did back then. He or she may be able to help you clear out the cobwebs and aid you in recalling old goals and dreams that you haven't thought about for years.

If your children are interested, share your high-school photos with your children. If nothing else, they will get a good laugh looking at your hairstyle and the clothes you wore.

Questions to Ask Yourself

To further jog your memory and help you identify with your daughter, ask yourself the following questions and write the answers in a journal.

- How is my life today different from what I imagined it would be when I was an adolescent?

- Did I have the support of my parents in my decision making? How did my parents' support or lack of support make me feel?

- Did my parents listen to me and encourage me to achieve my own goals?

- If you are a mom: How was my relationship with my mom?

- If you are a dad: Did I have any sisters whom I observed while growing up? If so, what was their relationship like with their mom?

- If you are a dad who did not have any female siblings: What was my wife's relationship like with her mom? What does she remember about her father's role?

- In what ways did I value myself then? To what did I link my self-esteem during adolescence? And do these links still exist today?

- How would I rate my own self-esteem as an adolescent and as an adult (optimal, satisfactory, or low)?

Take some time to think about these questions before you answer them. Writing in a journal will help.

Gathering all this information about your history should bring up some feelings from the past. Don't try to remember and grapple with everything all at once—think of this as a process. Take fifteen or twenty minutes each night for a few weeks to peruse your high-school photos and souvenirs and write in a journal about your experiences. When you focus on your old feelings from that time, you will have just a small glimpse of what your daughter is experiencing in her adolescence.

Reevaluate Your Beliefs

Now that you have connected with some of your feelings from adolescence, begin to think about the values and principles you had back then. How do they differ from the values and principles you have now as a parent?

Write down the values and principles you live by now. Ask yourself what is most important to you about being a parent. Share these beliefs with your children and spouse frequently.

Writing down your values and beliefs helps you reaffirm the boundaries you will set for your daughter at home, as well as your own boundaries. Keep in mind that the boundaries you are modeling for your daughter every day will help her to establish her own. In addition, asserting your family's values will let your daughter know what you expect of her and of everyone else in the family, and it will help you to stand firm when disagreements arise and she tries to wear you down to get her way.

Your children may laugh at your guidelines, but know that you are helping them to establish their own boundaries and formulate their own values. If your daughter challenges what you have written, do not get angry—at least she has read them. This challenge may be your daughter's way of showing you that she is trying to formulate her own belief system. Use this opportunity to discuss your values. Do not panic if she strays from your values. Instead, stay connected! Ask her to explain her position, and reinforce your position if necessary. Remember, consistent messages over time have a way of sinking in.

Can You Identify with Any of These Scenarios?

The following are discussions of several common causes of unnecessary conflict between parents and daughters. Now that you have begun your soul-searching to enable you to begin relating to your daughter from her perspective, read about the causes of unnecessary conflict below and see if you can identify your actions in any of them. If so, make a conscious effort to change your behavior. This will show your daughter that you care for her and save you unnecessary heartache and stress in the very near future.

Preferential Treatment or Double Standard

Do you treat your sons differently than your daughters? Are you tougher on the oldest child than her younger siblings? Girls tell me that situations like these drive them crazy and can cause unnecessary conflict.

Do you find yourself applying a double standard to your sons and daughters, thinking, "Boys will be boys," or "He can do that because he is a boy"? Doing so will continually irritate your daughter. When I have talked to parents about this double standard, they have said that they use it because they want to keep their daughter safe. Girls protest the use of the double standard because in their limited life experience they see it as simply unfair. The teen may think she is infallible and may not consider the possibility of rape, assault, pressured sex, or pregnancy. Without understanding their parents' desire to protect them, adolescent girls will respond angrily to the limits placed upon them, asking "Why don't you trust me?" A similar expression of anger from your daughter does not necessarily mean you should change your mind, but it does mean that you should take a closer look at the situation and explain your position to her.

Here is an example of a conversation that may lead to conflict:

◉

Daughter   *Why can Steve go to the concert but I can't. You don't trust me! You always let him go places but you never let me do anything.*

Parent   *Honey, it's not you that I don't trust. It's all the other people out there that I don't trust. And, well, your brother is a boy so I don't worry about him as much.*

Daughter   *Well you should trust my judgment about handling those people. I'm not a baby anymore.*

Parent   *You say you're not a baby anymore, but you sure are acting like one. I said no! And that is final! End of discussion.*

Daughter   *I hate you! (Stomps out the door.)*

◉

Be aware that telling your daughter she cannot do something her brother does because she is a girl may create feelings of betrayal. Try to avoid the "because he is a boy" explanation. Instead, help her to understand your concerns about her safety. Ask yourself whether you are being realistic about the issue. Discussing different scenarios with her and role-playing what she might do in dangerous situations may prepare her. Handling it in this way may help you feel more at ease about her physical safety. Remember, parenting is a balancing act, and when you place limits on your teenagers they will most likely challenge (or even disobey) you. Be sure you have a clear and reasonable explanation, and consider offering an alternative.

Now let's see an example of communicating effectively.

◎

Parent	*You're correct. You're not a baby anymore but I am worried about what might happen to you.*
Daughter	*Ugghh! Nothing is going to happen!*
Parent	*Look, you are obviously upset and frustrated. I can see that you want me to trust you to take care of yourself. I'm willing to sit down and talk to you about other solutions when you calm down and are ready to talk.*

◎

One parent explained to me that he was very worried about his sixteen-year-old daughter's safety when she went to a concert with some of her friends. He wanted to say that she couldn't go, but he was allowing his fourteen-year-old son to go with a group of friends, so he knew that he couldn't keep his daughter from going. The alternative that he came up with was to have the group of girls meet at their house before the concert. There he handed out his business card with his cellular phone number to each girl to call in the event of an emergency that evening. "Many of the girls thought I was so weird for handing out my business card, so I tried to make light of the situation. My goal was to help ensure my own daughter's safety. I wasn't as concerned with my son's safety at the concert because there was a parent going with the group and, well, I hate to say it, but he is a boy."

A parent of three girls suggested, "If your daughter wants to go to the shopping center with her friends to hang out, but you believe this is inappropriate because it is unsafe, then offer her an alternative. Having her friends come over to your house to hang out may be an alternative. She may not like this choice but at least you have given her an option."

Limiting Her Dreams and Goals

You can affect your daughter's belief in herself and her abilities when you apply a double standard for reasons other than safety concerns. For example, if your daughter approaches you and tells you she wants to be an electrician and you respond, "That is a man's job. Why don't you consider being a schoolteacher instead?" you are telling her to limit her goals and dreams. You are essentially saying that, regardless of her abilities, her options are limited because she is a woman.

Consider this story about an African American woman, now in her late thirties. Once, when she was an adolescent, she was in the family car with her father and she told her dad that she wanted to become an officer in the Navy. In the 1960s the idea of such a thing would have been thought preposterous. Few women and probably no African American women held high-ranking positions in the Navy at that time. Her father could easily have told her that this was an unrealistic goal for her, but instead he encouraged her and never once made her feel as if she could not achieve this goal. In 1998 she was the highest-ranking female officer in the Navy. Imagine how different her life would have been if her father had persuaded her that she didn't have a chance to reach her goal.

Competition

On the whole, our society encourages competition. Your daughter encounters competition at school, in social settings, and at home. She competes with her siblings for her parents' attention. She may even compete with her mother for her father's attention.

If a mother is not confident in her relationship with her husband, and her husband gives his love and attention more readily to the daughter, the mother and daughter may find themselves competing with each other. This situation is especially likely to occur when the wife does not express her feelings to her husband. Because the mother and father are not conscious of the family dynamic and do not deal with the real issue at hand, all of the relationships involved suffer unnecessarily.

Another potential problem caused by competition may occur if the mother has based her self-esteem on her own external appearance. As the years pass and her daughter matures into a beautiful girl, the mom may start to compete with her daughter for the attention of others. One teen complained that her mother was constantly trying to wear her clothes. By wearing her daughter's clothes and attempting to sustain her youthful appearance, she was taking attention away from her daughter and creating unhealthy competition. A daughter needs her mother to be an authority figure, not one of the girls. If the latter describes you as a parent, you may need to explore your feelings of competitiveness and determine their source.

Friend versus Parent

Parents often struggle with the question, "Can I be my daughter's friend as well as her parent?" One mom suggested, "Ask yourself what is your definition of a friend. If your definition is someone who accepts the other person for who they are, treats them with respect and dignity, and is there for them when they need someone, then there is nothing wrong with being a friend to your daughter. But if by friendship you mean sharing all your most intimate thoughts and feelings with her and allowing her to do things or say things because you are afraid of hurting her feelings, then no, it is not healthy to be your daughter's friend in this sense."

As girls mature, the friend-versus-parent issue becomes harder to puzzle out. Psychologist Gabriella Bentley has the following advice: "Although your daughter is almost an adult and can react like a companion, avoid the temptation to talk to them about your problems as well as your feelings in areas that might unsettle them. Examples of these areas are your sex life, relationship with partner, or secret fears."

In adolescence your daughter needs an authority figure who is consistent and compassionate. She needs someone who will listen and someone she can look up to and emulate. She needs someone she can count on to love her unconditionally. She needs someone who will set and enforce appropriate boundaries so she learns the difference between right and wrong. Giving her the structure and support that she needs through adolescence without being her "friend" may help you develop a friendship with her that is reciprocal when she is older and more mature.

Jealousy

If you find yourself being continually angry with your daughter and you cannot figure out why, ask yourself if you could be jealous. Are you jealous of her relationship with your husband? Are you jealous of the opportunities your daughter has? Are you jealous of your daughter because you gave up so much when you became a mother, and now your daughter is getting to do things you never got to do? Feeling jealous of your daughter could be a signal that you have deeper issues to uncover and work through in order to make way for a loving, long-lasting relationship with her. Reflecting on your child-hood and significant emotional events in your life may help you figure out what these issues are.

Unlived Life of the Parent

The unlived life of a parent can affect a child in many ways. Suppose your daughter has an interest in sports and you have always thought you could have been a good athlete if you had had the right coaches. You support her and encourage her to develop her skills. But somewhere along the line your daughter decides she does not want to play sports. When she tells you this, you respond by saying how disappointed you would be if she gave up. So, out of guilt, your daughter continues to participate, but she would rather spend her time doing something else.

This scenario can cause unnecessary conflict because of the expectation placed on the young girl that is not consistent with the expectations she has for herself. In the long run, the daughter never benefits from being made to feel guilty. In my experience, girls who engage in activities in order to please a parent do not have fun when they participate and feel that they are wasting their time. Parents should encourage, not force, their daughter's participation in extracurricular activities according to the girl's expectations and goals, not their own unfulfilled desires. In the past when I have had athletes come and tell me that they want to quit the team because they do not enjoy participating but that their parents will not let them, I ask them to think about the following questions:

❀ Do you think that when you are older you will regret your decision?

❀ Are you quitting because of what someone else thinks or is this a decision you have made on your own?

❀ What will you do instead of participating in this activity?

❀ What will you do instead to help you achieve the goals you have for your future?

It is important to be in tune with your daughter's goals and dreams. I generally do not advocate quitting an activity once it's begun, but if the only reason the daughter is participating is to please a parent, then that problem needs to be addressed.

If you are unsure whether your daughter is participating in an activity simply to make you happy, just ask her. Listen to her spoken answer, but watch her nonverbal response as well. If she has difficulty making eye contact with you when you discuss the topic, or if her physical response does not match her verbal response (for example, she says she is happy but her head is down and her voice sounds sullen), then there is most likely inconsistency between what she is telling you and what she is actually thinking or feeling.

Why Do They Want to Grow Up So Fast?

If you are a parent who worries about your daughter growing up too fast, you are not alone. The important question to ask yourself is where these concerns come from. Perhaps you are worried that she is exposed to more adult situations than you were at her age, and you want her to just be able to enjoy being a child. This is an understandable concern; staying connected with her and discussing these issues may help ease your mind. If, however, you are feeling insecure because your daughter is growing up and you are afraid she will not need you anymore, then this may signal that you have linked your self-esteem to your role of parent.

Growing up should not be looked at as something to dread, but instead as a time to savor. Allow your daughter to enjoy her journey through adolescence by being her safety net. Guide her and help her feel secure about herself. Check in with her often to make sure she feels heard, respected, and valued.

Power Struggles

Is your daughter's room a mess? Does she constantly leave late for school or make you late to your appointments? Is she driving you crazy because she doesn't listen and just doesn't seem to care? Does she go out at night and refuse to tell you where she is going or whom she is going with? Does it bother you that she continually disagrees with you?

If you answered yes to any of the above questions, then you may be involved in a struggle for control and power. The best advice from parents and therapists is to choose your battles carefully. Does it really matter that your daughter's room is not clean? If your daughter knows that this annoys you, she may be leaving it a mess on purpose. This may be something she feels she should have control over, and, in fact, she is right. Her room is her own space, and as long as hygiene is not a problem, she should be able to keep it as she likes. Give your daughter control over as many decisions as you can. If you take her power away by always forcing rules upon her and making decisions for her, then she may rebel because she needs to have some control over her life. A mom of a seventeen-year-old told me, "Once I relinquished some control and adjusted the rules of our house according to her age, she seemed less likely to purposely make me late for appointments or do things deliberately to make me angry. I found that when I didn't give her some control she resisted almost everything I did or said."

In addition, ask yourself whether you are feeling that because she is not listening to you, your daughter values you less, and whether you are reacting to these hurt feelings by becoming angry with your daughter. You may feel that in order to keep control in your own life you must try to win every battle. If you feel this way, take a look at your own life and see why you are holding on so tightly to power and control.

Dealing with Menopause during Adolescence?

So your daughter is experiencing hormone changes, resulting in mood swings and unpredictable behavior. As if that's not enough, her mom is dealing with her own mood swings and hot flashes as she goes through menopause. Conflict may arise when a mother is dealing with her own emotional symptoms as a result of menopause. To help decrease unnecessary conflict, a mother should become aware of what is going on in her own body, acknowledge her symptoms, and learn as much as she can about managing her emotional state.

In this case, the best option may be for the mother to simply be aware of her menopause-related difficulties and discuss these with her daughter. A mother in her mid-fifties with a teenage daughter revealed that she found her "change" easier to deal with after she discussed with her family what her needs were. She simply said that she was experiencing some difficulties and needed their support. This mom also reported that showing her family she would be there for them despite the occasional hot flash made "all the difference in the world in my relationships with my children."

◉ ◉ ◉

Warning Signs

How do you know when your daughter is in trouble? Adolescence is characterized by extreme highs and extreme lows, so how can you tell when to be concerned about your daughter?

In general, there are basic warning signs that indicate a teenage girl is having difficulties.[1] These warning signs are not evident in every child in every situation, but the presence of any or all of them should send up a red flag for parents to take notice.

❀ If your daughter is **moody** at times, be slightly concerned, but more than likely her moodiness is simply typical adolescent behavior. Nevertheless, watch for other signs of a problem, such as seeming consistently down, depressed, or upset. This may signal to you that something is going on that warrants further attention.

❀ Excessive **anger** toward parents, other family members, or friends may signify a deeper fear or problem.

❀ **Withdrawing** from parents and friends or outside activities usually indicates trouble.

❀ **Slipping grades** can signal difficulties. Especially when accompanied by withdrawal from friends and family, falling grades should not be ignored. This could indicate that your daughter is falling into a depressed state, is losing sight of her future, or other problems.

❀ **Excessive weight loss or gain** in a short time can be a red flag. Accompanied by an obsession with food or avoidance of food, excessive weight loss may indicate a potential eating disorder. Excessive weight gain may signal that your daughter is having trouble dealing with problems. Instead of talking about or working to fix what is bothering her she may be turning to food to comfort her and avoid emotional pain.

❀ **Promiscuous behavior** shows parents that their daughter may not be feeling competent or confident in herself. Perhaps she is trying to gain acceptance and competence by acting like the females on television and in movies who get the guy because of their appearance and what they "put out." Seeking physical intimacy by dressing a certain way, or acting a certain way in order to feel loved, begins a detrimental cycle.

The above are just a few warning signs that should alert

you to potentially bigger problems. Keep in mind that you have to put aside the distractions of your own hectic life to recognize what may be subtle signs. If you do not make a conscious effort to become aware of your daughter's state of mind, you will miss an opportunity to help her through a very difficult time. If the signs go unnoticed, the further your daughter will fall, and the harder it will be to bring her back to a healthy mindset.

Unhealthy as it may be, at some level your daughter's destructive behavior works for her. Through her behavior she receives a secondary benefit (for example, she may be finding the control she seeks or the love she feels she is missing). The longer the problem is allowed to continue, the more difficult it will be for you to convince your daughter that something else, something more positive, will meet her needs more effectively.

As you read this chapter you will notice a common thread linking all of the conditions discussed: low self-esteem and lack of healthy coping mechanisms. These can lead your daughter down a dangerous and unhappy path. Staying connected with her through adolescence has been proven to decrease her chances of traveling down the wrong road.

We are going to discuss in detail some of the problems or conditions your adolescent daughter or her friends may experience. The following are the most common problems. If you suspect your daughter is struggling with any of these problems, do not hesitate to contact your pediatrician and/or a family therapist to help remedy the situation. These things can happen to your daughter if she is struggling and does not know a healthier way to deal with her pain.

The participation of youth in positive activities and the formation of close attachment to family, school, and community have been associated with positive outcomes for children.

America's Children Key National Indicators 2000

Depression

Mary Pipher, author of *Reviving Ophelia,* describes depression as "grieving for the lost self."[2] Young girls suffering from depression internalize their emotional struggles. Depression often manifests as feelings of worthlessness, inadequacy, and incompetence. Everyone feels down occasionally; this is normal as long as you can lift yourself back up. Depression results when you feel you just cannot get yourself going anymore. Young girls who are depressed can exhibit unwarranted anger, lethargy, and apathy toward life.[3]

Trying to meet society's expectations, their parents' expectations, and their own expectations can be debilitating for children. It is no wonder they get depressed these days. We require our children to meet certain expectations, but we also need to teach them healthy coping mechanisms to use when the pressure gets too great, and model healthy behavior for them so they have a good example to follow. Teach your children to recognize the signs of depression discussed above so that they can head it off at the pass or ask for help when needed. Feeling worthless, inadequate, and incompetent for two weeks or more may indicate that intervention is needed.

Depressed individuals may experiment with unhealthy outlets in order to gain a sense of competence or to ease their uncontrollable pain, especially when they see no other healthier options. A depressed adolescent may turn to drugs, alcohol, or food to ease her pain. Promiscuity may result from depression and wanting validation from an outside source. Some adolescents may attempt suicide if they feel there is no way out (or if they feel there is no other way to get the attention of the adults in their life).

If you recognize the warning signs of depression in your daughter, discuss with her what you see. Remind her that help is available. Try to help her replace the negative thoughts that are going through her mind with positive, constructive thoughts. This is the first step to stop negative feelings from consuming her. Low self-esteem and the lack of healthy coping skills can lead to depressive episodes. Encourage your child to develop healthy ways of dealing with stress, fear, and anger (and model these coping mechanisms for her as well) so she feels she has options when she is down.

If you feel your daughter is depressed and she has not responded to your attempts to help, seek the aid of a trained therapist or counselor to help you understand what you are dealing with and how to cope with it.

Whether she seems depressed or not, using effective communication techniques, approach your daughter and give her an opportunity to open up to you. For example, when just the two of you go to a movie or go shopping, inconspicuously ask her about her feelings.

Parent	*I haven't had a chance to talk to you in a while. We both have been so busy. How is your friend Jenny doing?*
Daughter	*Fine. She's fine.*
Parent	*So Jenny's fine, huh? Well, what did you think of the girl in the news the other day? You know, the girl who lost her boyfriend in that accident?*

If you talk with your daughter about risky behavior, and she doesn't respond positively to the direct approach, bringing up a current event involving someone her age, talking about a television show she watches, or talking about the movie you just saw will help break the ice and her guard somewhat. Asking her if she is depressed will inevitably result in one answer: "I'm fine."

Daughter	*I didn't hear about it. What happened?*
Parent	*Well, the girl was about your age. She was in a car accident and her boyfriend, who was driving, died. She must be devastated.*
Daughter	*Whoa. That would be horrible.*
Parent	*The girl became very depressed after the incident. The article talked about depression and its symptoms. Do you ever get depressed?*
Daughter	*Well, yeah, sometimes I feel like I'm depressed. But not 'cause of anything major like that, but I just get bummed, you know?*
Parent	*Yeah, I get bummed too sometimes. What do you do to get yourself out of it?*
Daughter	*Sometimes I don't know what to do. Most times it just goes away. There is this girl at school that I know. You have to promise not to freak out or anything, but she, you know, cuts herself.*
Parent	*She cuts herself? (Holding back the unconscious reaction.) Do you think that's a good way to deal with your feelings?*

◎

This conversation could go on from here to talk about healthy coping mechanisms. Please refer to the examples of coping mechanisms that were discussed in chapter 4 for ideas.

Another conversation might go as follows:

◎

Parent	*Hi, honey. Wondering if I could come in and talk to you for a minute?*
Daughter	*Yeah, whatever. (Looking down, avoiding eye contact.)*
Parent	*(Using rapport-building skills to subtly show your daughter that you are trying to make a connection with*

her.) I just wanted to come by and see how you're doing. You seem down lately.

Daughter   I'm fine. (Still looking down.)

Parent   (Gently touching your daughter's shoulder, pausing, and making eye contact for a few seconds in silence if your daughter looks up.) I get the feeling that something is bothering you because, even though you say you're fine, you haven't been acting as though you're fine lately. And I'm not pushing you to talk if you don't want to but I just want to let you know that I'm here when you need me. If you do choose to talk to me then I promise I won't be judgmental or freak out.

Daughter   (No response.)

Parent   And if you don't want to talk to me for whatever reason I would like you to consider talking to a counselor at school or a teacher you like. Because if you don't, I am going to be attached to your hip and annoy the heck out of you until you do (using humor to connect with your daughter). Because I love you and I'm concerned.

○

Writing a letter or starting a parent-child journal will open the lines of communication. Contacting the school and asking a trusted teacher, coach, or counselor to check in with your daughter can give you some peace of mind that she is at least talking to an adult. Ask the individual not to mention that you contacted them and to approach your daughter as if they had noticed something was bothering her. (The teacher, coach, or counselor will probably have noticed the same symptoms that you have.)

Eating Disorders

Studies indicate that up to 6 percent of girls in the United States have an eating disorder.[4]

Family and personal traits can predispose an adolescent girl to developing an eating disorder.

Family factors:

- Perfectionistic and highly critical parents
- Over-involved parenting or enmeshment
- Under-involved parenting or little emotion expressed in the family
- Chaotic family function
- Disengaged family function
- Family history of eating disorders
- Family history of obesity
- Family history of mood disorders
- Family history of substance abuse
- Caucasian ethnicity; middle to upper class (anorexia)

Personal factors:

- Perfectionism
- Difficulty expressing feelings and emotions
- Low self-esteem
- Dissatisfaction with body image
- Being age thirteen to eighteen
- Obesity
- Frequent dieting
- Using unhealthy weight-control measures such as taking laxatives or diet pills
- Early dieting

- ✿ Early maturation
- ✿ Early dating
- ✿ History of depression, anxiety, substance abuse, physical abuse, or sexual abuse
- ✿ Feeling of lack of control in life

I became extremely concerned about the prevalence of eating disorders when talking to one teen about the topic. She admitted to me that she had been anorexic for a short time but was able to pull herself out of it when she started to feel that food was controlling her life. I asked her why she thought she had fallen into the food trap in the first place. She responded by telling me that in health class, when the topic of eating disorders was discussed, it sounded as though giving up food for a while was a viable option for losing weight. This young woman felt that eating disorders were almost glorified, and not condemned, in her class. She said, "Everyone tried it after we studied it in health class. Everyone was either throwing up or starving themselves for weeks."

The media's constant supply of unrealistic role models for young girls, discussed in chapter 5, may be a contributing factor to the development of eating disorders in girls. Parents must arm their daughters with the necessary information to recognize that what they see on television and in magazines is not real. Sitting down with your daughter and discussing these facts will help her understand that what she sees in the media is far from the norm.

The average American model stands 5 feet 11 inches tall and weighs 117 pounds. The average American woman in 1996 stood 5 feet 4 inches tall and weighed 140 pounds.

Anorexia Nervosa

Anorexia is an eating disorder that involves starving oneself, in some cases to death. Statistics reveal that 15 to 20 percent of anorexics eventually die from the toll the profound weight loss takes on their bodies.[5] Anorexia typically begins in early adolescence. Girls begin to be obsessed with food and dieting and start to hate their bodies. They experience a severe self-induced weight loss. Anorexics feel just right or even fat when they are actually extremely thin.[6]

There are many speculations about what causes a child to become anorexic. Each individual has her own underlying conscious or unconscious reasons. One theory Dr. Julie White, author of *Building Self-Esteem in Your Daughter*, mentions is that girls become anorexic because they are ambivalent about growing up and becoming an adult female. By controlling their weight to an extreme, their breasts do not fully develop and their bodies remain small. It's almost as if they are saying, "I'm not here. I do not exist. I am not important."

Another reason cited by many experts is lack of control. An anorexic may feel that she does not have any control over her life. Dr. Pipher states, "She is essentially saying (to her parents) 'you see, you can't control my every move' and to society, 'I can be thinner than you want me to be. I am in control of what I eat and you can't make me eat more.'"[7]

Who becomes anorexic? Statistics reveal that anorexia is most prevalent in Caucasian families of bright, high achievers. The authors of *Bulimarexia* report that anorexics come from upwardly mobile families in which moms are overinvolved and dads are preoccupied with work out of the home.[8]

Anorexics have low self-esteem and wish to gain approval. If a girl has lost weight at a young age, this weight loss is often noticed and complimented by peers and even family members.

Boys may begin to notice her and she becomes convinced that thinner is better.

Girls in the early stages of anorexia may frequently say they just ate or aren't hungry. They tend to obsess about exercise, food, and dieting. As the disease progresses, physical signs manifest in a distended abdomen and fine, lifeless hair. Menstruation ceases. Their body becomes weak and more susceptible to infections.

Even if she does not become anorexic herself, your daughter will run across someone who is anorexic or who has attempted starving herself to lose weight. The best way to help her recognize that this is not an appropriate weight-loss method is to talk with her about it. Give her a book that you feel is appropriate for her to read on the topic and then discuss it with her. One mother with two adolescent daughters said she gave her daughter certain sections of *Reviving Ophelia* to read and afterward they discussed this issue. Two years later when the daughter was fifteen she came back to her mom and thanked her for sharing that information with her. Her daughter's friend was now struggling with anorexia and she felt better prepared to face this situation since she had been exposed to this information two years before.

If you believe your daughter is anorexic, forcing her to eat is not the answer. She will undoubtedly resist your attempts to control her eating. Consult your pediatrician and arrange for your daughter to see a counselor and a nutritionist. The hardest part for parents who have a tendency to be controlling is to give up control and to allow their daughter to make herself better. The therapist, nutritionist, and physician can help her realize that anorexia is not her friend. The adolescent girl has allowed this horrible disease to infiltrate her psyche. She believes that being anorexic will make her beautiful and feel wonderful. Your daughter has to activate the anorexic within herself in order to heal and resolve the underlying issues.

Bulimia

Bulimia is characterized by the binge-purge cycle. Bulimics will uncontrollably stuff themselves with food and later vomit, use laxatives, or fast to keep from gaining weight or to lose weight. Bulimia, unlike anorexia, tends to begin in later adolescence, sometimes during college. The actual number of girls practicing bulimic behaviors is difficult to determine because bulimics tend to hide their secret well. They maintain a relatively normal weight and their behaviors are often inconspicuous. Mary Pipher states that these girls "have sold their soul[9] for the perfect body." Bulimia, like anorexia, is a result of our society's obsession with thinness and the perfect body.

Dieting behaviors and concerns about body size increase with age for girls. Almost half of eleven-year-old girls and two-thirds of fifteen-year-old girls in the United States reported that they were dieting or felt they should be on a diet.

1997–98 survey National Institute of Child Health and Human Development.

Bulimics have low self-esteem and some essential personal needs that are not being met, so they turn to binging and purging for control, acceptance, and achievement. At first, controlling the binge-purge cycle can be accomplished, but most bulimics eventually find themselves unable to control the compelling feeling to purge. This activity fills a need for the young girl. The immediate gratification from food leads to purging so that the bulimic can feel relaxed and not guilty about the food she ate. But following the purge she may feel shame as a result of her actions.

Physical signs and effects of bulimia include the following:

❀ Enamel on the teeth may be eroded due to the stomach acids that are thrown up.

❀ The index finger may have a scar from contact with the stomach acids as a result of habitually sticking her finger down her throat. Esophageal lesions can occur.

❀ Gastrointestinal problems are common.

❀ Purging can create chemical imbalances that may lead to a heart attack.

If you suspect that your daughter is a bulimic, contact your pediatrician and seek out a qualified therapist and nutritionist for your daughter. They can assist your daughter to regain control and stability in her life. You can encourage your daughter to find ways to validate herself instead of looking for validation elsewhere. In addition, you can take a look at your life and see if you are modeling effective and healthy coping mechanisms. If not, do a little work yourself and you will help your daughter tremendously. Overeaters Anonymous is also a good resource to contact if your daughter is having trouble controlling her eating.

Overeating

Overeating is also a very common eating disorder that some girls develop in adolescence.

At an age when acceptance from peers is very important, being overweight can be horribly painful for your daughter. Unfortunately, our society is not very kind to overweight individuals. We tend to judge them as lazy, dumb, and unmotivated. If our children are overweight they feel inadequate. And kids who are not overweight do not seem to hesitate to make fun of overweight individuals. Most kids do not have enough life experience to know that those who make fun of others are insecure themselves. Overweight children internalize the experience, which causes pain and causes them to eat more.

Overeaters tend to have low self-esteem. They turn to food to satisfy their need for love, acceptance, and approval. A team consisting of a pediatrician, counselor, and nutritionist can often help an overweight child. If you are a parent of a child who overeats, do not fool yourself and think food is the issue. Your child is almost certainly having difficulty dealing with some underlying issues, which can be examined in family and individual counseling.

Even though the underlying cause of overeating may not be the food itself, it is still a good idea to pay attention to what foods you keep in the house. Below are a few suggestions for reducing your child's temptation to overeat at home.

- ❀ Keep healthy food around the house.
- ❀ Get rid of the chips and candy bars.
- ❀ Encourage physical activity by going biking or walking together.
- ❀ Teach your daughter to eat to live, not live to eat.
- ❀ Limit the amount of time your daughter spends watching television or sitting in front of the computer.

When your older teen starts driving, talk to her about resisting the temptation to "drive thru" at her favorite fast-food restaurant. Help her become conscious of what she is putting in her mouth and teach her that convenience is not a smart substitute for health.

Avoid asking your child if she is hungry. Instead, ask her if she is satisfied or full. When you ask her if she is hungry, even if she isn't actually hungry your question may trigger a feeling of hunger. Asking her if she is full will help her focus on the feeling of being full instead of hungry.

Utilizing effective com-munication techniques may help you uncover the reasons for your child's overeating. Instead of calling her fat or telling her to stop eating junk food, help her find the patterns related to her overeating. Ask her if she eats when she is bored, stressed, afraid, or upset. Help her adopt healthier coping mechanisms to change these patterns. Journaling can be an effective way for your daughter to uncover the emotional issues connected to her overeating.

With all eating disorders, parents first need to address the child's self-esteem issue. Parents should examine the role they play in the situation. Are you physically or emotionally disconnected? Ask your child. She will tell you what you are doing wrong. Put aside your reaction to her criticism and meet your child's needs. Model appropriate coping mechanisms. Stop talking about your weight. Teach your children not to judge others by their looks. Teach your daughter to see her own body in a healthy, realistic way.

Self-Mutilation

Self-mutilation (also called self-injury or self-harm) is increasing all over the world. This behavior includes but is not limited to cutting, burning, or scratching oneself as a way of dealing with inner pain and turmoil. It is an extreme form of turning on oneself to release the buried despair inside. Girls engage in self-mutilation when they have no other means of coping with their problems.

What benefits do these girls get out of hurting themselves? One girl told me, "It was the only thing I could do to calm myself down. I guess it relaxes me." After an apparent suicide attempt another girl confided, "I really didn't want to die. I just needed to get the pain out of me. I wanted to bleed it out." The physical pain she inflicts on herself may give the girl a feeling of euphoria due to a release of endorphins. One teen told me, "I kind of feel like I'm floating when it's over. I almost feel numb." One teen described self-mutilation as a way of dealing with her feelings of being out of control. Not until she went to therapy did she realize that cutting herself was a choice she was making.

Self-mutilation is distinguished from attempted suicide in that when a person attempts to commit suicide she wants to end all feelings. When a person who self-harms hurts herself she wants to release the feelings so she can feel better.

Low self-esteem, a lack of healthy coping mechanisms, and not being allowed to feel or express their emotions can lead to girls harming themselves. In some cases, self-mutilation has been identified in victims of sexual assault or sexual abuse. But Dr. Pipher has good news, stating, "Most young women respond quickly to guidance about how to stop this behavior and develop more adaptive coping mechanisms."[10] They can learn the benefits of talking about their pain and coping with the stress they are dealing with.

The fact that self-mutilation has become more common is just another indication that using effective communication, developing healthy coping skills, and encouraging your daughter to feel and express her feelings are a vital part of parenting. By doing so you can steer your daughter away from these unhealthy and sometimes deadly behaviors.

Seek help from a professional as soon as you notice any signs of self-mutilation. These signs can include burn marks or successive cuts on the body. These injuries may be found on the wrists, thighs, or abdomen but are not limited to these areas. The sooner the intervention is started the easier it will be for your daughter to stop this behavior.

Unhealthy Relationships

Relationships become important early on in the life of a girl. Who her friends are, how many friends she has, and whether she is popular seem to carry a great deal of weight for the adolescent. One thing that is not so evident, and is often overlooked, is the importance of the relationship with her family at this time. As a young girl reaches this age she begins to take her family, especially her parents, for granted. She is confident that they will always be there, so she goes out to develop new relationships with peers, both boys and girls, and seemingly leaves her parents behind.

This is the time when some parents also seem to pull away. They believe that their daughter needs to separate from them in order to be independent, so they disconnect from the relationship. Sometimes the opposite is true; parents are so hurt or frightened that their daughter does not seem to need them anymore that they pull the reins too tight, causing rebellion and resentment.

However independent they seem, adolescent girls still need the support, guidance, and love of their parents so they feel secure and are less likely to get involved in unhealthy behaviors or relationships.

Unhealthy Relationships with Peers

Unhealthy relationships with peers can erode the self-esteem of your daughter, especially because adolescents tend to link their self-worth to their ability to be accepted by their peers. What should parents do about these unhealthy relationships? First, recognize that abusive relationships can occur with boys or with girls. Certainly physical abuse is less likely to occur in your daughter's relationship with another girl, but verbal and emotional abuse happens in some relationships with either sex.

Next, parents should teach young girls that just because certain behaviors do not leave visible marks (as with emotional and verbal abuse), this is still abuse and should not be tolerated. As a matter of fact, the marks we cannot see, the injuries to our heart and soul, are the most difficult to heal.

Any relationship that involves a lack of respect toward your daughter should concern you and her. However, you may have no idea what is going on in your daughter's relationships. You may think her boyfriend is the nicest and sweetest thing on this earth because he acts like such a gentleman around you. Or you may be comfortable with her friends because they seem so polite when you are around. But to your daughter, at times, these boys and girls may be just the opposite.

Depression, withdrawal, anger, and apathy could be indications of an unhealthy relationship. Pay attention, keep the communication going, and stay connected to your daughter. Then you'll be able to see the signs if they are there.

Why does your daughter stay in an unhealthy relationship, especially if it involves any kind of abuse? Low self-esteem. One girl told me, "I didn't think I could do any better." Another said, "I didn't think I deserved any better," and "He was jealous because he loves me." And yet another stated, "I just wanted someone to love me."

Early in the relationship girls may equate attention and jealousy with love. Gavin De Becker, author of *Protecting the Gift,* sums it up by writing, "The fact that a romantic pursuer is relentless doesn't mean you are special. It means that he is troubled." By staying in these relationships the adolescents are fulfilling their need for attention, even if this attention is negative. These girls unconsciously seek any kind of attention that will make them feel loved.

The pattern can be interrupted by helping girls eliminate their connection between love and abuse and by teaching them to develop new internal feedback mechanisms so they will equate love with more positive attention. When they accept and love themselves first and create boundaries so that others will respect them, they can move out of this type of relationship and never return. Changing a young girl's perception of her relationship may require intervention by a therapist or counselor.

Is She is in An Unhealthy Relationship?

Here are warning signs of an unhealthy relationship to share with your daughter:[11]

- ❀ He or she monopolizes your time and attention.
- ❀ He or she says that he or she loves you very early in the relationship.
- ❀ You are required to check in with him or her frequently.
- ❀ He or she is extremely jealous and possessive.
- ❀ He or she is aggressive in other areas of his or her life.
- ❀ He or she blames you for bringing out the worst in him or her.
- ❀ He or she tries to isolate you from your friends and family.
- ❀ He or she calls you names and embarrasses you in front of others.
- ❀ He or she has an explosive temper.
- ❀ He or she uses drugs or alcohol excessively.
- ❀ He or she persuades you to do something you feel is against your values.

Every parent should go over this list with his or her daughter early in her adolescence, encouraging her to take a good look at her current relationships—including friendships with other girls.

Substance Abuse

Alcohol Abuse

Alcohol is the most widely used drug among youth today. Thirty percent of twelfth graders, 25 percent of tenth graders, and 13 percent of eighth graders reported having had at least five drinks in a row at least once in the previous three weeks.[12] Forty percent of ninth graders said that they had tried alcohol before the age of 13 and had used it in the past month.[13]

> "Alcohol is the number one drug of choice among our nation's youth. Yet the seriousness of this issue does not register with the general public or policy makers."
> —Enoch Gordis, MS, Director of the National Institute on Alcohol Abuse and Alcoholism (NIH)

Sixty-six percent of youths who heavily drank alcohol in the past month had also used illicit drugs in the past month.[14]

Many people with whom I have discussed this topic (both adults and teens) insist that experimenting with alcohol is a normal occurrence. However, the following statistics speak for themselves: among teenagers in the United States who binge drink, 39 percent say they drink alone, 58 percent drink when they are upset, 30 percent drink when they are bored, and 37 percent drink to feel high. Thirteen- to fifteen-year-olds are at a high risk to begin drinking. Binge drinking at least once during the two weeks before a survey was reported by 16 percent of eighth graders, 25 percent of tenth graders, and 30 percent of twelfth graders.[15]

Illicit Drug Use

Illicit drugs include marijuana, cocaine (including crack), heroin, hallucinogens (LSD, PCP, Ecstasy), amphetamines, and psychotherapeutic drugs (nonmedical use).

> A survey by the Health and Human Services Division revealed that 18 percent of female teens and 39 percent of male teens say it is acceptable for a boy to force sex if the girl is stoned or drunk.

Among youths aged twelve to seventeen years, 9.7 percent had used an illicit drug in the thirty days prior to the interview. The average age to begin smoking marijuana in 1999 was seventeen years. The average age to start cocaine use was nineteen years.[16]

Girls are more likely than boys to report use of psychotherapeutic drugs (nonmedical use of pharmaceutical drugs). This does not include over-the-counter medications.

According to the longitudinal study by Michael Resnick, author of *Protecting Adolescents from Harm,* home environment plays a major role in whether a teen uses illicit drugs. When adolescents do not have access to drugs and alcohol in the home, they are less likely to use them[17].

> Children who report strong communication with their parents are less likely to drink.
> Centers for Disease Control

Nicotine Use

Cigarette smoking among youths has dropped in recent years, but still poses a national health risk. It is estimated that more than five million of today's underage smokers will die of tobacco-related illnesses. Rates of smoking for males and females are similar according to the National Center for Health Statistics:

- 5 percent of eighth-grade females smoke versus 6 percent of males
- 12 percent of tenth-grade females smoke versus 12 percent of males
- 19 percent of twelfth-grade females smoke versus 18 percent of males
- Approximately 52 percent of youths who smoked cigarettes in the past month had also used illicit drugs in the past month.[18]

Inhalant Use

More than two million youths (9 percent of twelve- to seventeen-year-olds) report using inhalants once in their lifetime.[19]

Inhalants include:

❀ glue

❀ gasoline

❀ lighter fluid

❀ spray paints

❀ correction fluids

❀ degreaser

❀ cleaning fluid

Feelings of personal connectedness to family and school play a crucial role in protecting young people from cigarette, alcohol, and marijuana use as well as violence, suicide, and early sexual activity.

Today's Issues (National Institute of Child Health and Human Development) 8 (August 1998), 1–2.

Why?

Why do adolescents get involved in drugs at an early age? Depression, low self-esteem, and peer pressure are a few of the reasons I have observed. It's common for teens to believe, "Nothing bad can happen to me," and "Everyone is doing it."

Youngsters who are depressed often use alcohol and drugs to medicate themselves or ease their pain. They lack the appropriate coping skills that would help them to express and manage their feelings.

The American Academy of Pediatrics reports that adolescents who are less likely to use alcohol or other drugs are close to their parents emotionally. Other deterrents to alcohol and drug abuse include parents who provide sound, consistent guidance, and siblings who are intolerant of substance abuse. Adolescents who are expected to comply with clearly stated rules of conduct are also less likely to use drugs and alcohol.

A recent study by professors at Columbia University reported that teens who have an active spiritual life, either religious or nonreligious, are half as likely to become alcohol and drug addicts or even to try illegal drugs.

Protect your children: give them the tools to resist using and abusing these substances. As we have discussed, building optimal self-esteem, enforcing clear boundaries, modeling appropriate behaviors, and teaching your children healthy ways to cope with their problems through effective communication are all key factors in keeping your child from abusing these substances.

Promiscuity

Promiscuous behavior can be a sign of many different issues or problems. The adolescent may believe that in order to be loved by someone she must have sex. She may link sexual attractiveness to feeling confident, important, or worthy. She may crave and need physical contact and/or emotional contact in order to feel better about herself.

Promiscuous behavior usually reflects a feeling of low self-worth in an individual. Whatever the reason for the promiscuity, the probability remains that the adolescent is attempting to fill a void in herself through an external source, which usually only ends up hurting her and supporting her feelings of inadequacy. Her feelings of worthlessness as a result of her actions may lead her to continue pursuing the very actions that continually cause her pain.

One young woman in her early twenties described her experience. "When I got to university I was feeling very unsure of myself and I felt very inadequate. I tried to make myself feel better by being with a different guy every week. This somehow, in the short term, gave me confidence about myself, but this feeling didn't last. Because after I was with a guy I would feel worse about myself knowing that I shouldn't have slept with him in the first place. It was like I kept doing the same thing over and over until I finally realized how my life would be ruined if I continued."

This type of behavior can also put girls at risk for infectious diseases, teenage pregnancy, and death as a result of diseases such as HIV.

Talk to your daughter about promiscuity, sexually transmitted diseases, and teen pregnancy. Educate her on the reasons girls may become promiscuous. Asking for her opinion and her thoughts on the subject will help her to begin developing her own set of values for herself. You can share your thoughts as well. Cutting out articles and taping them to her bedroom or bathroom mirror is a good way to get her thinking about this topic. Then discuss these issues later. Also try to make a point of bringing up promiscuous activities shown on television shows and in the movies and ask her opinion about what the women portrayed on television and in the movies are doing.

Teen Pregnancy

Are you concerned about your daughter becoming sexually active at a young age or even possibly becoming pregnant? This is a realistic concern, although teen pregnancy rates have dropped in the United States in recent years. In the year 2000 there were 157,209 births to girls 15 to 17 years old, which is approximately 27 births per 1,000 girls.[20]

What can you do to prevent teenage pregnancy? Adolescents who reported strong emotional ties with their family and school were more likely than their peers to delay sexual intercourse.[21] The World Congress of Gynecology and Obstetrics reports that formal education about sex, open communication about sex, and easy access to educational services and birth control have resulted in a dramatic decrease in teen pregnancy in countries such as Switzerland.

Keeping your daughter involved in extracurricular activities can lower her chances of becoming pregnant as a teen. It is well documented that girls involved in athletics are less likely to practice unhealthy, risky behaviors. Help your daughter find activities in which she can gain a sense of accomplishment and increase her self-confidence. Meet her need to feel loved. Some teenagers who choose to become pregnant report that they wanted a baby so they could experience unconditional love.

Finally, although it may be uncomfortable for both parent and child, talk about sex with your teenager. Bring the subject up when the two of you are alone in a casual way. Discussing your values and beliefs with your daughter about sexual activity is essential. Making your beliefs known to her may deter her from having sex at an early age.

Suicide

According to the American Association of Suicidology, in 1999 girls were three times more likely to attempt suicide than boys, but boys were four times more likely to complete a suicide. Authors Tonia K. Shamoo and Philip Patros state that the following warning signs may indicate that your child is troubled by suicidal thoughts:[22]

- ❀ change in eating and sleeping habits
- ❀ withdrawal from friends, family, and regular activities
- ❀ violent actions, rebellious behavior, or running away
- ❀ drug and alcohol use
- ❀ abrupt, prolonged changes in behavior
- ❀ persistent boredom, difficulty concentrating, or a decline in the quality of schoolwork
- ❀ frequent complaints about physical symptoms, often related to emotions, such as stomachaches, headaches, and fatigue.
- ❀ statements such as "I want to kill myself," "I won't be a problem for you much longer," "Nothing matters," or "No one would care if I wasn't here anyway"
- ❀ giving away valued possessions
- ❀ sudden cheerfulness after a period of depression

Be observant of any signs listed above as well as any signs related to depression. Any time an adolescent says, "I want to kill myself," always take the statement seriously. Talk to your pediatrician for referrals to a psychiatrist or other physician. Counselors and therapists should also be included in the treatment team.

Don't be afraid to talk to your daughter about suicide or depression. Ignoring it will not make it go away. And talking about it will *not* put ideas in her head. By expressing your concern, you will show her that someone really does care about her.

When approaching your daughter about suicide, you must listen to what she has to say. Encourage her to express and feel all of her feelings. If she has shown any of the warning signs listed above and you are concerned about her, refrain from telling her all the reasons she should not commit suicide, and by all means do not tell her that her feelings are foolish or that she is being silly. Instead, reassure her that she can be helped and that she will have your support at all times.

Follow through by finding help for your daughter. Let your other kids know that they can reach out for help as well. Crisis hotlines are available in your community and they can be found in your local telephone directory. These resources can be helpful to all of the members of your family.

A Note about Therapists and Counselors

Encourage your daughter to attend counseling if necessary. And if you are finding it difficult to cope with the stress of parenting, needing counseling is nothing to be ashamed of. No book on parenting can answer all of your questions; sorting out your thoughts with a therapist can be very beneficial.

It is also important to be realistic. If you or your daughter seeks counseling and you or she finds that the person you are seeing is not right for you, then try someone else. It is important that the person attending counseling sessions be comfortable with her therapist. If you feel uncomfortable, you will be less able to open up and share your feelings. Finding the right professional, someone whom you or your daughter can relate to, will make all the difference in the world.

Many different types of therapists use many different techniques, such as cognitive behavioral therapy, Time Line Therapy™, Neurolinguistic programming, and hypnotherapy. Each therapist can offer a unique array of techniques to assist you and your daughter. Inquire about what techniques the person you are going to see uses and whether he or she has experience working with adolescents and families. The most important criterion is that your daughter feels a positive connection to the therapist.

Staying connected with your daughter throughout adolescence will allow you to notice any warning signs when they appear. Knowing what to do when these signs appear will enable you to intervene when necessary.

◎ ◎ ◎

Author's Notes

Chapter One

1. John Coleman and Leo Hendry, *Nature of Adolescence,* 3rd ed. (London: Routledge, 1999), 8 and Lynda Madaras, *What's Happening to My Body* (New York: Penguin Books, 1989), 102-5.

2. The discussion regarding the onset of menstruation is referenced in Jennifer Grimwade, *The Body of Knowledge* (Australia: William Heninemann, 1995), 72-73.

3. The average age to begin menstruation is twelve or thirteen. Grimwade, *Body of Knowledge,* 72-73.

4. Boys are usually two years behind girls. Grimwade, *The Body of Knowledge,* 151.

5. Theodore Lidz, *The Person: His Development throughout the Life Cycle* (New York: Basic Books, 1968).

6. Mary Pipher, *Reviving Ophelia* (New York: Ballantine, 1996), 57-58.

7. Dave Begel, *Bringing Up Emily* (Chicago: Turnbull and Willoughby, 1986).

8. A complete separation from one's daughter creates disconnection instead of establishing the safety net necessary to effectively support the adolescent girl.

9. Elizabeth DeBold, Marie Wilson, and Idelisse Malave, *Mother Daughter Revolution* (New York: Addison-Wesley Publishing, 1993), 19-20.

10. Lidz, *The Person: His Development throughout the Life Cycle.*

Chapter Two

1. Published in Sean Covey's, *Seven Habits of Highly Effective Teens* (New York: Simon & Schuster, 1998).

2. Stephen Covey, *Seven Habits of Highly Effective People* (New York: Simon & Schuster, 1989).

3. The components of empathic listening were adapted from Covey, *Seven Habits of Highly Effective People,* 18.

4. Covey, *Seven Habits of Highly Effective People.*

5. Catherine Bush, telephone conversation with author, 20 April 2001.

Chapter Three

1. Allen Ivey and Mary Bradford Ivey, *Intentional Interviewing and Counseling* (Pacific Grove, CA: Brooks/Cole Publishing, 1999), 57–71.

2. Ivey and Ivey, *Intentional Interviewing and Counseling,* 64.

3. Phil McGraw, *Life Strategies* (New York: Hyperion, 1999), 91–92.

4. This passage is based on the benefits of empathic listening in Covey, *Seven Habits of Highly Effective People.*

Chapter Four

1. Susan Baile, Ph.D., *Building Self-Esteem in Your Child* (audiotape) (Boulder, Colo.: Career Track, 1992).

2. The diaphragmatic breathing exercise is a technique the author used in her practice as a physiotherapist. A reference to a similar exercise is in Daniel Girdano, George Everly, and Dorothy Dusek, *Controlling Stress and Tension* (New Jersey: Prentice Hall, 1995).

Chapter Five

1. American Association of University Women, *Shortchanging Girls, Shortchanging America* (Washington, D.C.: American Association of University Women, 1991).

2. Referring to British educators, "they know that boys do better than girls on self-esteem questionnaires." Christina Hoff Sommers, *The War against Boys* (New York: Simon and Schuster, 2000), 161.

3. The definition of self-esteem is based on conversations with and observations of adolescents and parents, and on the author's personal ideas.

4. Baile, *Building Self-Esteem in Your Daughter.*

5. Dr. Jan Yager, *Friendshifts: The Power of Friendship and How It Shapes Our Lives* (Stamford, CT: Hannacroix Creek Books, 1999).

6. "Pain is inevitable; suffering is optional" is based on a quote by a guest on the *Oprah Winfrey Show*, 30 November 2000.

7. Julie White, *Building Self-Esteem in Your Daughter* (audiotape) (Boulder, Colo. Career Track, 1995).

8. "Through Dad's Eyes," *Milwaukee Journal Sentinel*, 11 February 2001, Lifestyle section.

Chapter Six

1. D. Kim Openshaw, Ph.D., *Building Children's Self-Esteem* (Logan, UT: Utah State University, 1999).

Chapter Seven

1. These sources of conflict were identified during interviews with mothers with at least one daughter from 1995 to 2000. Also included were results from surveys given to over two hundred adolescent girls from 1999 to 2001.

2. Greater intensity of conflict was more likely between mothers and daughters than between other relationships in the family. L. Steinberg, "Reciprocal relations between parent-child, distance, and pubertal maturation." *Developmental Psychology* 24 (1988), 122-28.

3. The advice in this section is based on the author's own experiences with her father and interviews from 1995 to 2000 with fathers who had at least two daughters.

4. "Through Dad's Eyes."

5. This section was inspired by Sarah Ban Breathnach, *Simple Abundance* (New York: Warner Books, 1995).

Chapter Eight

1. This list of warning signs is adapted from American Academy of Child Adolescent Psychiatry, *Your Adolescent* (New York: HarperCollins, 1999), 209, 213-14 (Suicide and Depression).

2. Pipher, *Reviving Ophelia*, 150.

3. The material on depression was influenced by Pipher, *Reviving Ophelia*, 150, and Tonia Shamoo and Phillip Patros, *Depression and Suicide in Children and Adolescents* (New York: Simon and Schuster, 1989), 81-90.

4. Based on data from the Eating Disorder Association (QLD) Resource Center.

5.   Based on data from the Eating Disorder Association (QLD) Resource Center.

6.   White, *Building Self-Esteem in Your Daughter.*

7.   Pipher, *Reviving Ophelia,* 174.

8.   Marlene Boskind-White and William White. Jr., *Bulimarexia* (New York: Norton, 1991).

9.   Pipher, *Reviving Ophelia,* 170.

10. Pipher, *Reviving Ophelia,* 157-158.

11. This list was influenced by information presented on *The Oprah Winfrey Show,* "Abusive Teen Dating," 16 April 1999, and the author's own observations since 1987.

12. National Center for Health Statistics, *National Health Survey 2002.*

13. Centers for Disease Control.

14. National Household Survey on Drug Abuse 2000.

15. Health and Human Services Division.

16. National Household Survey on Drug Abuse 2000.

17. Resnick MD, Bearman PS, Blum RW, et al. *Protecting Adolescents from Harm: Findings from the National Longitudinal Study on Adolescent Health.* (JAMA, 1997)

18. National Household Survey on Drug Abuse 2000.

19. National Household Survey on Drug Abuse 2000.

20. Health and Human Services, *America's Children 2002.*

21. *Study of Adolescent Health,* Journal of the American Medical Association, September 1997.

22. Shamoo and Patros, *Depression and Suicide in Children and Adolescents,* 91-104.

Index

Contact Information

Please refer comments or queries to Stacey Roberts via her website at www.breastfairy.com, or via email at breastfairy22@hotmail.com. Watch for the new website, www.understandinggirls.com. Ms. Roberts gives seminars and presentations regarding the topic of raising adolescent girls, as well as motivation, business consulting, sales, marketing, and personal breakthrough sessions. Her consulting company, Life Strategies Unlimited, is recognized internationally. Please contact her for more detailed information.

Mailing addresses:

Australia: 4 Coronga Crescent, Killara, NSW 2071

United States: Positive Image Publishing, 6311 West North Avenue, Wauwatosa, WI 53213

Stacey Roberts Ph.D.-C.